QUR'AN
MANUSCRIPTS

Calligraphy, Illumination, Design

Colin F. Baker

The British Library

First published 2007 by
The British Library
96 Euston Road
London NW1 2DB

Text © 2007 Colin F. Baker
Illustrations © 2007 The British Library Board
and other named copyright holders

British Library Cataloguing
in Publication Data
A Catalogue record for this book is
available from The British Library

ISBN 978 0 7123 0689 8

Designed by Andrew Shoolbred
Printed and bound in Italy by Trento S.r.l.

ABOVE Ornamental upper panel from the incipit page of a
17th-century Chinese Qur'an written in *sini* script.
BL Or.15604, ff. 1v-2 (detail).

HALF-TITLE PAGE Ornate marker inscribed in *kufic* script from
the 14th-century Mamluk Qur'an of Sultan Faraj ibn Barquq, Cairo.
BL Or.848, f. 26v (detail).

TITLE PAGE *Shamsah* (sunburst) medallion from a 16th-century
Qur'an, Afghanistan or possibly India.
BL Or.11544, ff. 3v-4 (detail, enlarged).

FRONT JACKET The incipit page from part nine of Sultan Faraj ibn
Barquq's thirty-volume Qur'an.
BL Or.848, f. 2r.

BACK JACKET Ornamental marker from Sultan Faraj ibn Barquq's
thirty-volume Qur'an. BL Or.848, f. 26v (detail).

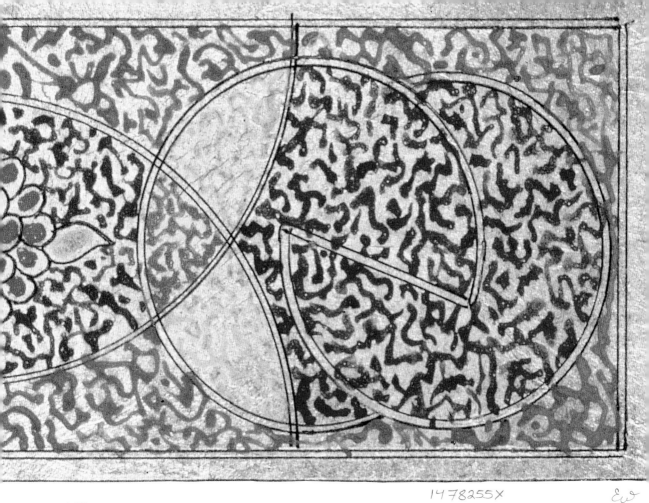

1478255X   Ew

Contents

Introduction

Islam is one of the great monotheistic religions of the world together with Judaism and Christianity. Though they have a common belief in one God, each has its own sacred book at the core of its religion. The Hebrew Bible and the New Testament are respectively the holy books of Judaism and Christianity, while the Qur'an is the holy book of Islam. With millions of Muslims worldwide, it is unquestionably one of the world's most influential texts. For those who live by its teachings, the text is considered the actual word of God and, in accordance with tradition, is read aloud; indeed, the word Qur'an derives from the Arabic verb 'to recite'. The religion – Islam – takes its name from the Arabic word meaning 'submission to the will of God'.

According to the Muslim faith, the teachings of Islam contained in the Qur'an were revealed to the Prophet Muhammad in the Arabic language via the archangel Gabriel. Muslim tradition also has it that Muhammad received the divine revelation over a period of time, between 610 AD and his death in 632, and that he received the first of these divine messages in the cave of al-Hira', while wandering alone outside Mecca in the western Hijaz region of the Arabian Peninsula. At first his message was ill-received by the merchants and the religious authorities of the city, who objected to his religious and social teachings.

2 OPPOSITE Decorative text page containing part of chapter one, *Surat al-fatihah* ('The opening chapter'), from a 16th-century Qur'an copied in Afghanistan or possibly India. BL Or.11544, f. 4r.

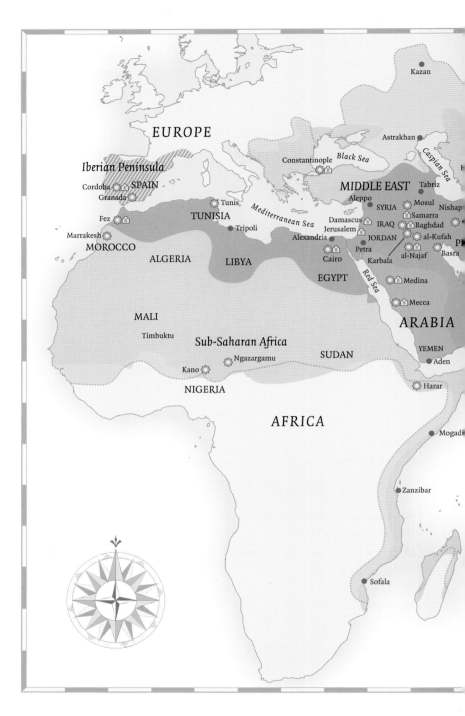

3 RIGHT Map of the Islamic world, from the 7th to 18th centuries.

So great was the opposition and hostility, that Muhammad and his group of followers were later forced to migrate from Mecca to Yathrib, now known as Medina, where his message was more readily accepted. The migration – in Arabic the hijrah – took place in the year 622. This is a significant date in the Muslim calendar, for the date of the migration, traditionally 16 July 622, marks the start of the Muslim era; all dates in the Muslim calendar are reckoned from it.

Initially the divine revelations were committed to memory, transmitted

MONGOLIA

Kashgar

Samarqand

CENTRAL ASIA

Beijing ●

rat

HANISTAN

Lahore ●

TIBET

Xian

Shanghai ●

Delhi

CHINA

at

Bihar ●

Indian Subcontinent

INDIA

Bay of
Bengal

South China
Sea

bian Sea

Goa ●

Calicut ●

Malay Peninsula

Malacca ●

SUMATRA

BORNEO

INDIAN OCEAN

Macassar ●

JAVA

The spread of Islam

by 632, at the death of the Prophet

by 750, at the end of the Umayyad dynasty

by 1500

by 1700

under Christian rule by 1500

centres of learning

major mosques

from believer to believer. At the time of the revelations, the Arabs were mainly
a tribal and nomadic society in which the spoken word was given precedence
over the written as a means of communication. Reliance on memory, however,
is hardly the most secure way of preserving and ensuring the accuracy of a divine message, particularly for future generations. This consideration was
acutely pertinent to Muhammad's early followers. Accordingly, the first caliph,
Abu Bakr (r. 632–4), who succeeded Muhammad on his death, ensured that

the revelations were recorded in writing by ordering Muhammad's secretary, Zayd ibn Thabit, to compile them in book form. Tradition has it that the original compilation of the text was collected not only from the oral recollections of Muhammad's early followers, but also from early transmissions written on fragments of such readily available materials as parchment, papyrus, stone, camel bone, palm leaves and leather.

Within twenty years the number of Qur'an manuscripts in circulation hugely increased due to the spread of Islam into Iraq and Syria under Abu Bakr, and then into Egypt, North Africa, and Persia under the second caliph, 'Umar ibn al-Khattab (r. 634–44). Given this situation, it became urgently necessary to establish a canonized text which would preserve the sanctity of the message and fix an authorized spelling of the text for all time. This task was promptly undertaken in the year 651 by order of the third caliph, 'Uthman ibn 'Affan (r. 644–56); and the definitive canonical text, as recited today in mosques and privately throughout the world, was produced. The text is formally arranged in 114 *surahs* or chapters. Chapter one apart, these are traditionally arranged in order according to length, from the longest to the shortest, and not in the sequence in which they were revealed. Most of the shorter chapters were revealed to Muhammad in the hostile environment of Mecca before he migrated to Medina, whereas the longer chapters were revealed after he had settled there. With the exception of chapter nine, each chapter begins with an expression of piety, the *basmalah*, which reads 'In the name of God, the Merciful, the Compassionate'.

Being the supreme book of the Islamic faith, the Qur'an is central to the Muslim way of life. Together with the *Hadith* – the collected traditions based on the sayings and actions of Muhammad and his followers – it influences all aspects of the daily life of the individual believer whether at home, in the mosque, the Qur'an school (*kuttab*), or the religious academy (*madrasah*). For Muslims living outside the Middle East it is often their first exposure to the Arabic language, while for all Muslims it is the primary text from which Arabic is taught. Indeed, it is incumbent on Muslims, whichever part of the world they live in, to learn to read and recite the Qur'an in Arabic.

Just as the text of the Qur'an is considered sacrosanct and infallible, the physical form of the book is also treated with reverence. Belief in the word of God and respect for the object containing the word of God – the Qur'an – are therefore inextricably related, unifying Muslims in all parts of the world. Devotion to the book is exemplified by the way Qur'an manuscripts have been devoutly and assiduously copied throughout the centuries, exhibiting diverse features of styles in calligraphy, illumination, physical format and page layout, which often reflect their place of origin and date of production. From the late seventh to the nineteenth century, the writing of Qur'an manuscripts was undertaken, as one would expect, in predominantly Islamic parts of the world and in countries with large Muslim communities. Today, with the geographical spread of Islam covering Arabia and the Near and Middle East, North Africa and Spain, sub-Saharan Africa, Iran and Central Asia, the Indian subcontinent, South East Asia and China (fig. 3), and with the availability of printed copies throughout all these areas, the copying of Qur'ans by hand is no longer necessary, but nevertheless continued where traditional calligraphy is still practised.

To a great extent, the history of Qur'an manuscripts is the history of Arabic script. For, in copying the Qur'an, calligraphers have made use of a wide range of styles, reflecting stages in the development of Arabic writing. Written from right to left, the Arabic language consists of twenty-nine letters and belongs to the Semitic family of scripts which include among others Hebrew, Aramaic and Syriac. A common feature of all these languages is the fact that their alphabets are composed almost entirely of consonants, vowel signs being added only later to facilitate reading.

The origins of Arabic script can be traced back to early Phoenician script in the twelfth century BC, which influenced, among other Semitic scripts, the script used for the Aramaic language. A version of this Aramaic script – called Nabatean Aramaic, because of its association with the official language of the Nabatean kingdom of Petra in Jordan (c. 100 BC–c. 100 AD) – was first used for writing Arabic in the fourth century AD. By the middle of the sixth century, however, Nabatean Aramaic had itself evolved through a number of transitional stages to what is recognizably the Arabic script of the Qur'an. The significance of the Qur'an in the development of Arabic script is reinforced by the fact that until the sixth century Arabic writing was mainly on stone, very few examples of which have survived to this day. The fact that Muhammad received his message in the Arabic language, and that the Qur'an was later committed to writing in the Arabic script, gave the language and its script a heightened level of religious significance and sanctity.

ولا من منهم فليسكن

اﻻ ان اﻻ تعمر ولا

منهم فليعمرن

خلق الله ومن

فيه السكن

From the early stages

The earliest Qur'an manuscripts were produced in the mid-to-late seventh century AD (first century hijrah), although it is difficult to be precise about their date, due to the fact that ancient copies from this period have not survived intact and exist only in fragments. The importance of these fragments cannot be overestimated as they provide the only available evidence for the early development of the written recording of the Qur'an text.

The ma'il Qur'an

The largest fragment of consecutive text is from the so-called ma'il Qur'an which dates from the eighth century and, as far as can be ascertained, was produced in the Hijaz region of the Arabian Peninsula, the area which includes the holy cities of Mecca and Medina (fig. 5). The word ma'il itself means 'sloping' and refers to the sloping style of the script. This is one of a number of early Arabic scripts collectively named 'Hijazi' after the region in which they were developed. The ma'il Qur'an contains over two-thirds of the Qur'an text, making it an almost complete codex and one of the oldest Qur'ans in existence.

The ma'il Qur'an is penned on parchment, the generic term for writing material prepared from the skins of sheep, goats and calves. This material was

4 OPPOSITE An 11th-century Qur'an, from Spain or North Africa, written on parchment in maghribi script, with vowel signs indicated in red and other spelling symbols in blue-green and saffron.
BL Or.11780, f. 65r (enlarged).

5 OPPOSITE AND BELOW The British Library's *ma'il* Qur'an, Arabia, 8th century. Among the most ancient copies of the Qur'an, containing over two-thirds of the complete text, it is one of the largest known fragments of an early Qur'an in the *ma'il* script. See examples of the letters *alif* (below left) and *ya'* (below right).
BL Or.2165, f. 77r.

popular for Qur'an codices of this period because of its flexible yet durable qualities. Papyrus, though mostly used in Egypt and in plentiful supply, was not generally used for Qur'ans. It was usually preferred for legal and commercial documents which were written in a scroll format. Muslims adopted the codex for their holy book, presumably because it was portable and more manageable, and possibly because they were influenced by the Coptic Gospels which were also in this format. The codex – *mushaf* in Arabic, which in current usage can refer to any volume of the Qur'an – was originally a collection of sheets of parchment placed between two boards. Each double sheet was folded into two leaves, which were assembled into gatherings, then sewn together and bound as quires into a book or codex. The text is always presented on the page in a single-column block, not in columns, as is often found in the codices of other cultures within the region, the Hebrew Bible and the Greek New Testament, for example. Unlike the Qur'an, these sacred writings were originally in scroll format, the form which later influenced the multi-column layout of their manuscript pages.

The main characteristic of *ma'il* script is its pronounced slant to the right. It can also be recognized by the distinctive traits of some of its letters; in particular *alif* and *ya'* (the first and last letters of the Arabic alphabet). The *alif* does not curve at the bottom, it is rigid; on the other hand, the *ya'*, occurring at the end of a word, turns and extends backwards, frequently underlining the preced-

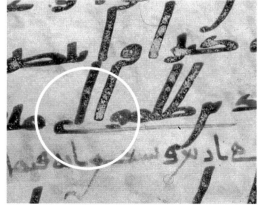

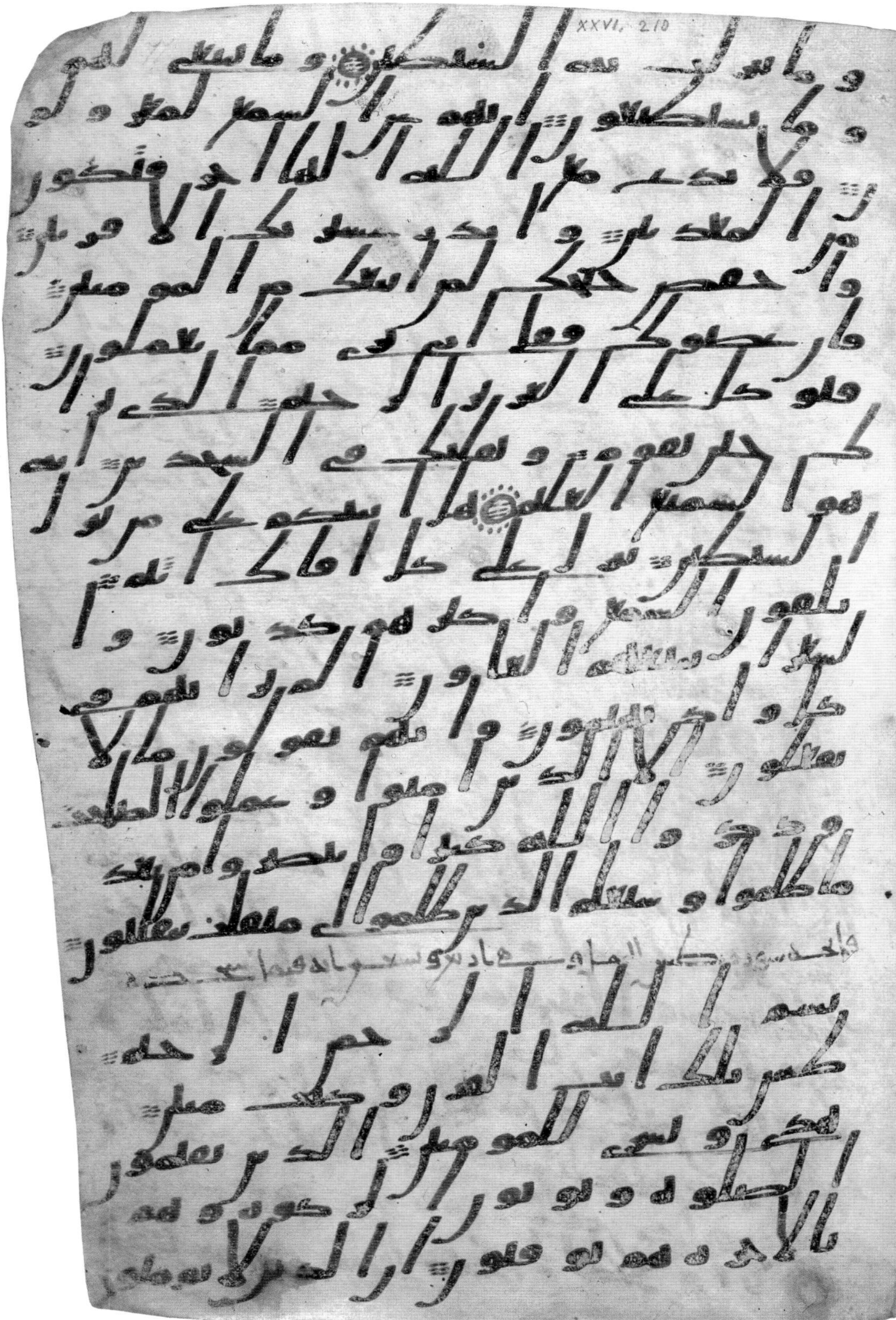
XXVI, 210

ing words. This early style of script is also notable for its lack of diacritical marks, that is, the spelling symbols which distinguish between letters of similar shape. In the ma'il Qur'an and other ancient fragments there are no vowel signs or other aids to pronunciation. In early Qur'ans the method for numbering verses is not fully developed. In the earliest fragments, such as the ma'il, the end of each verse is indicated by six small dashes in two stacks of three. A later development in the verse numbering of this Qur'an was the addition of red circles surrounded by red dots to mark the end of every ten verses (fig. 5, top line). Likewise, chapter headings were also added later in a different script and colour from the rest of the text. This is clearly evident because early Qur'ans usually distinguished between the end and beginning of chapters by leaving between them a recognizable space which could be filled in with a horizontal illuminated band (fig. 6). When chapter headings were later introduced, the wording stated the name of the chapter, the number of verses and whether the particular chapter was revealed in Mecca or Medina.

Kufic Qur'ans and the beginnings of illumination

The physical shape of the earliest Qur'an codices was vertical in format, as exemplified by the ma'il Qur'an. But, as demonstrated in early Qur'ans of the ninth and tenth centuries written in kufic script, choice of script can be seen to have had a major influence on the shape of the volume, which was now produced in a horizontal format (fig. 7). With its very short vertical and elongated horizontal strokes, the kufic style is certainly suited to the oblong format of Qur'ans produced in the Near East. This format is thought to have been originally inspired by the shape of unrolled papyrus scrolls, also possibly by the oblong wood and stone panels inscribed with Qur'anic quotations on the walls of mosques. The earliest examples of Qur'anic inscriptions in kufic script, dating from 692, appear on the Dome of the Rock in Jerusalem.

This strikingly angular script takes its name from the town of al-Kufah in southern Iraq, which was one of the earliest centres of Islamic learning and from where the script is believed to have been developed. Qur'ans in kufic script are organized in blocks, with the words of text often split between the end of one line and the beginning of another. Signs were introduced into the text as an aid to pronunciation. Representing an older system based on a method developed by the seventh-century founder of Arabic grammar, Abu al-Aswad al-

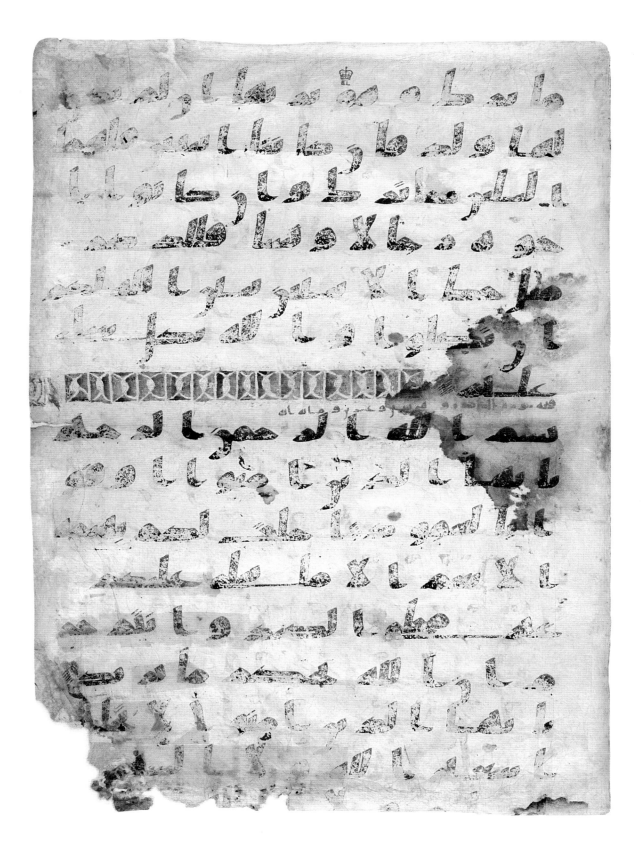

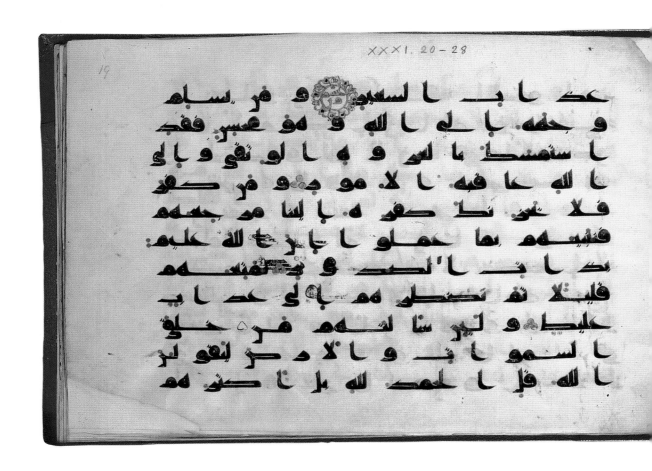

7 A 9th-century Qur'an, Near East, in horizontal format, written on parchment in *kufic* script, with red dots for vowels and green dots indicating the glottal stop. The large gold roundel marks the end of a tenth verse.
BL Or.1397, ff. 18v-19.

Du'ali, red dots were added to indicate vowels, with green dots to indicate the glottal stop (*hamzah*). In the eighth century, a system of short black diagonal strokes was further introduced to avoid confusion between similar-shaped letters. Credit for this system is attributed to al-Hallaj ibn Yusuf, a governor of the Islamic East during the Umayyad caliphate (661–750), who instructed pupils of Abu al-Aswad al-Du'ali to solve the problem.

These early *kufic* Qur'ans already exhibit the beginnings of those elements of illumination and decoration that were so eminently brought to perfection in later Qur'ans, giving the written word a heightened power and resonance. Since Islam does not approve of the representation of the human or animal form in religious contexts, Islamic art finds its ultimate spiritual expression in sacred calligraphy, the writing down of a holy text in a beautifully ornamented script. There can be no doubt that the Qur'an has played a pivotal role in the development of this art form. While beautifying the Qur'an manuscript can be considered as an act of religious devotion, the decorations on its pages have the additional function of facilitating reading. Hence, Qur'an illumination follows the structural division of the text, highlighting within the body of the text or in the margins, chapter headings, ends of verses, verse counts to mark the end of a fifth and tenth verse, the beginning of sections, and the fourteen points at which the believer should prostrate during the recitation of the Qur'an. In manuscripts from other cultures the opening pages, the headings of chapters and sections, and the initial letters are often illustrated. Since, however, there are no capital letters in Arabic script and illustration is forbidden, Qur'an illumination emphasizes key words and headings. These are generally illuminated in gold or other colours, or written in a different script from the rest of the text, and sometimes even with a combination of all three. Where illumination is

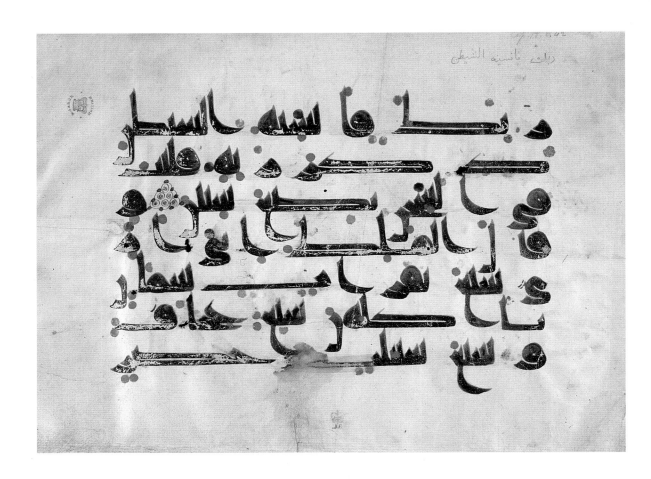

8 Detail of the ornamental letter ha' (third line) from a Qur'an in kufic script, 9th or 10th century. The pyramid-shaped ornament (top left) indicates the end of a fifth verse.
BL Add.11737, f. 3r.

present in early Qur'ans, as in the kufic, its role is clearly discernible. For example, the end of a fifth verse is marked by a gold ornamental letter ha', the letter ha' having the value of five in the Arabic alphanumeric system (fig. 8). In this system, known as abjad, each letter of the Arabic alphabet has been allotted a numerical value. Similarly, the end of a tenth verse is noted by a large roundel in gold, in which the number of the verse is inscribed in words (fig. 9); trefoils are used to form a pyramid of gold circles to mark the end of the other verses.

Eastern kufic

From the tenth century Qur'ans are once again being produced in a vertical format, thus underlining the relationship between the physical shape of the volume and the script of the manuscript. The return to the vertical was largely necessitated by choice of script, due particularly to the appearance of eastern kufic, first developed by the Persians, the letters of which are characterized by long upright strokes and short strokes inclining to the left. Specific styles were evolved within eastern kufic, such as Qarmatian (figs. 10, 11). The name of this style is possibly derived from the Arabic verb (qarmata) in an expression which suggests that the script is finer and that the letters are closer together. Further

developments in the notation of vowel signs were introduced into Qur'an manuscripts: the older system of red dots associated with Abu al-Aswad al-Du'ali was combined with the vowel signs – still in use today – developed by the eighth-century grammarian and philologist, al-Khalil ibn Ahmad.

Early naskhi and paper

While parchment was the favoured material for early Qur'ans, paper gradually began to be chosen as the preferred medium. A popular tradition has it that the art of papermaking came to Samarqand in Central Asia in the eighth century, having been extracted from Chinese prisoners captured during the Islamic invasion of Central Asia. Papermaking soon spread throughout the Middle East, paper mills being established in major centres in Iraq, Persia, Yemen, Egypt and Syria. The cities of Samarqand, Baghdad, Cairo and Damascus became renowned for paper produced to an exceptionally high quality. Although one might expect a sacred text to be written on costly parchment rather than paper, by the tenth century Qur'an manuscripts in the eastern part of the Islamic empire as distinct from the Islamic West (North Africa and Spain) were written only on paper, as were other Arabic manuscripts.

9 Detail of an illuminated medallion from a Qur'an in kufic script, 9th or 10th century. The large roundel (left) indicates the end of a tenth verse, with the Arabic word for 'ten' ('ashr) in gold.
BL Add.11737, f. 9r.

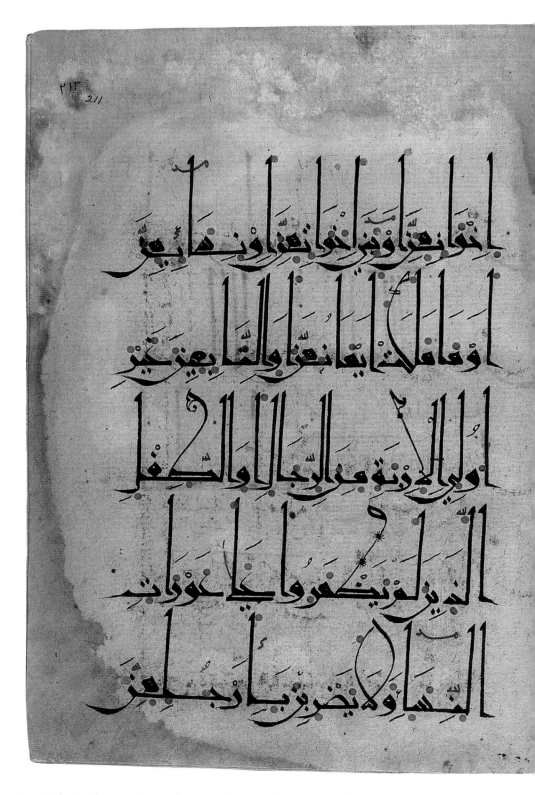

10 An 11th- or 12th-century Qur'an, from Iraq or Persia, written on paper in the Qarmatian style of eastern *kufic* script. The older system of red dots indicating vowels is combined with black vowel signs still in use today. BL Or.6573, ff. 210v-211.

Some of the earliest Qur'ans written on paper were penned in a cursive script, proportional in style, known as *naskhi* (*fig. 12*). While eastern *kufic* was used for copying the Qur'an text, the introduction of *naskhi* in the Islamic East from around the late tenth century may have also contributed to the re-adoption of the vertical format. Though *kufic* and an early type of *naskhi* were both concurrently in use between the eighth and tenth centuries, the latter was employed only in documents of an administrative and commercial nature and not for the sacred text. More fully developed in the tenth century by the Abbasid vizier and calligrapher Ibn Muqlah (886–940), and later perfected by Ibn al-Bawwab (d. 1022), the master calligrapher who continued his tradition, *naskhi* became one of the most popular styles for transcribing Arabic manuscripts due to its legibility.

The impact of early *naskhi* can be easily appreciated from its appearance upon the Qur'an page. A striking feature of the layout in such a Qur'an is the distribution of the space occupied by the script and the illumination, both being packed densely together within the text area, with marginal ornaments almost touching the area of the text in a way that is reminiscent of an overlapping chain. By the middle of the eleventh century, the relationship between *naskhi* and *kufic* can be seen to be one of contrast between text and ornament. *Kufic* was now an archaic script used only for ornamental purposes to inscribe the text within the illumination. Hence, in an eleventh-century Qur'an written in

11 ABOVE Detail of an ornamental chapter heading from a 10th-century Qur'an in eastern *kufic* script, Iraq or Persia. The chapter heading (centre), written in gold *thuluth* script extends into the margin to form a palmette (left). BL Or.12884, f. 122r.

12 OPPOSITE A Qur'an from Iraq or Persia, dated 427/1036, in early *naskhi* script written on paper. Small gold roundels within the text mark the end of each verse. The little palmettes in the margin, which are in the shape of the Arabic letter *ha'*, indicate the end of a fifth verse. The larger overlapping roundels mark the end of a tenth verse. BL Add.7214, f. 52v.

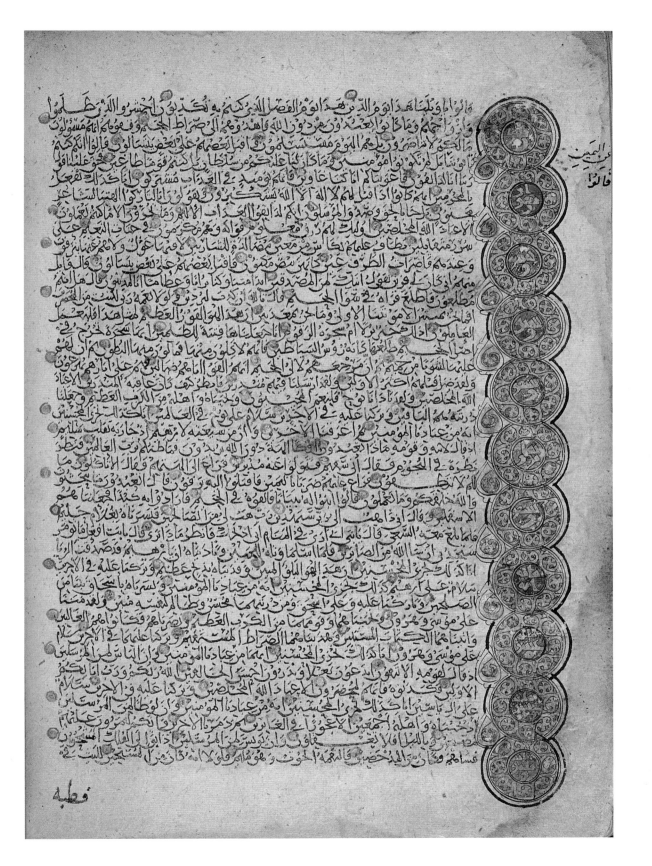

13 A 13th-century Qur'an, probably from Granada, written on parchment. The ornamental chapter heading (top left) is written in western *kufic* script, the text in *maghribi* script, with vowel signs in blue. This Qur'an was originally in sixty parts, of which this volume is part thirty-nine. BL Or.12523C, ff. 14v-15.

early *naskhi* script, the larger overlapping roundels marking the end of a tenth verse have their relevant verse number spelt out in *kufic*.

The Qur'an in the Islamic West

During the reign of the Umayyad caliphs (661–750) who ruled from Damascus, Islam spread west from Egypt to Libya, Tunisia, Algeria and Morocco. Expanding also into the Iberian Peninsula, Islam became the dominant power in Spain from 711 until the Christian re-conquest during the second quarter of the thirteenth century. Qur'ans from North Africa and Spain differ significantly from those produced in the Islamic East (fig. 13). One difference can be seen in their use of writing material. While parchment was no longer a material of choice in the Islamic East, the Islamic West continued to produce Qur'ans on parchment until the fourteenth century, no doubt because this region of the Islamic world was late in its introduction to paper manufacture. A regional style

of script also developed in the West with its own peculiar characteristics. This script, *maghribi*, named after the province of Maghreb in North Africa, became the accepted script for copying Qur'ans and other texts in North Africa, and by the twelfth century was also adopted in Andalusian Spain. A number of features differentiate *maghribi* from other Arabic scripts, particularly in the way the letters *fa'* and *qaf* are written. Its vowel signs are usually penned in red or blue, with the glottal stop also indicated by coloured dots. The characteristics of *maghribi* clearly show that its origins lie in western *kufic*, the regional version of *kufic* developed in Tunisia during the tenth century. This script can be recognized by its more rounded and deeper curves extending below the line, a feature which became a prominent characteristic of *maghribi* script. The interrelationship between these scripts is highlighted in the pages of a thirteenth-century Qur'an from Spain (fig. 13), which contrasts its ornamental chapter headings, written in gold angular western *kufic*, with its text in *maghribi*. The *maghribi* script in the main body of the text, with its sweeping curves below the line and the pronounced roundness and lengthening of some of its letters, gives these Qur'an pages the sense of space and movement associated with cursive scripts.

Qur'an formats

It should be noted that the script or format of a Qur'an did not determine the number of its volumes. Irrespective of shape, whether horizontal or vertical, Qur'ans could be in either one volume or in multi-volume sets. Of multi-volume Qur'ans, the thirty-volume set was the more usual; each volume contained a thirtieth of the text (juz'), following the traditional division of the Qur'an text into thirty sections. Thirty-volume sets became popular, because the whole of the Qur'an can be read completely during those months of the Muslim calendar which have thirty days, and especially during the holy month of Ramadan, one volume being recited each day. In addition, Qur'ans were copied in sixty parts, as the text is also traditionally divided into sixty equal sections (hizb). Seven-volume sets, each volume containing a seventh (sub') of the text, are also found but are very rare indeed.

Developments in illumination

From around the late tenth century onwards the development of scripts and formats was accompanied in both the Islamic East and West by a gradual movement towards a more elaborate illumination. This may have been due at least in part to satisfy royal or noble patrons who wished to endow a mosque or teaching institution with a Qur'an which would appropriately reflect their power and piety. Decoration and ornamentation became progressively complex, not exclusively within the text itself, but also in other parts of the volume such as the single or double frontispiece. These pages, designed with full-page illuminations, are sometimes referred to as 'carpet' pages since their appearance resembles oriental carpets (figs. 14, 15, 16, 17). Although carpet pages do not fall strictly within the realm of the sacred text, the illuminator was aware of the opportunity not only to display his artistry but also to set the sacred tone of the volume in order to prepare the reader mentally and spiritually for its contents. In architectural terms, opening a Qur'an volume might be compared to entering a sacred building, with the carpet page as the gateway or portal to the holy text itself. Its role is thus similar to that of the courtyard of a mosque, which, acting as a transitional link between the everyday world and the spiritual, helps the believer to achieve an appropriate state of mind and composure before entering the prayer hall. At the end of the volume a full-page illumination is also often found, thereby balancing the frontispiece both functionally and decoratively.

In Qur'ans, whether written in *kufic*, early *naskhi* or *maghribi* script, a number of design features characterize the full-page illuminations at the beginning or end of their volumes. Among these are the arabesques (interwoven flowing patterns of floral motifs), the geometric patterns highlighted in white ink, and the compartmentalized sections within a rectangular framework. As in decorations for chapter headings, a palmette was sometimes attached to the outermost border of the carpet page. Later, when carpet pages became even more elaborate, quotations from the Qur'an were inscribed on the upper and lower panels within the rectangular framework.

Traditionally certain Qur'an pages were treated more elaborately than others. For example, the opening pages immediately following the frontispiece – the first double page of text – were especially embellished. These opening text pages can be referred to as 'incipit pages'. While this term generally refers to the beginning of a major section of text in western manuscripts, it is particularly appropriate to the description of the decorated opening text pages in Islamic manuscripts, given their nature and design. For Muslims, the significance of this opening is that it contains the whole of the first chapter of the Qur'an, *Surat al-fatihah* ('The opening chapter'), the particular importance of which is its recitation during the five daily prayers. In multi-volume Qur'ans, the decorated incipit pages carry the opening of the relevant section. Other elaborately illuminated pages are generally found in the centre opening of the volume and also in the final openings containing the shortest chapters which, according to Muslim tradition, were revealed to Muhammad in Mecca.

14 Ornate frontispiece of a 10th-century Qur'an, probably from
Egypt, with arabesque decoration in gold and overlapping
chain-patterns in white. BL Add.11735, ff. IV-2.

15 Illuminated frontispiece of an 11th-century Qur'an, Iraq or Persia, with
the central geometric pattern highlighted in white. BL Add.7214, ff. 2v-3.

16 Decorative end pages of a 16th-century Qur'an from Morocco. BL Or.1405, ff. 399v-400.

17 The carpet pages designed by Muhammad ibn Mubadir, from volume one of Sultan Baybars' seven-volume Qur'an, dated 1305–06. The quotation in the panels is one of the most widely used in carpet pages and comes from chapter 56, verses 77–80: 'This is indeed a noble Qur'an, in a well-preserved Book, which none shall touch but the purified. It is a revelation from the Lord of the worlds'. BL Add.22406, ff. IV-2.

بِسْمِ اللَّهِ الرَّحْمَنِ الرَّحِيمِ

اقْرَأْ بِاسْمِ رَبِّكَ الَّذِي خَلَقَ ۞ خَلَقَ الْإِنسَانَ مِنْ عَلَقٍ ۞ اقْرَأْ وَرَبُّكَ

الْأَكْرَمُ ۞ الَّذِي عَلَّمَ بِالْقَلَمِ ۞ عَلَّمَ الْإِنسَانَ مَا لَمْ يَعْلَمْ ۞ كَلَّا إِنَّ الْإِنسَانَ

لَيَطْغَى ۞ أَن رَّآهُ اسْتَغْنَى ۞ إِنَّ إِلَى رَبِّكَ الرُّجْعَى ۞ أَرَأَيْتَ الَّذِي يَنْهَى ۞

عَبْدًا إِذَا صَلَّى ۞ أَرَأَيْتَ إِن كَانَ عَلَى الْهُدَى ۞ أَوْ أَمَرَ بِالتَّقْوَى ۞ أَرَأَيْتَ إِن كَذَّبَ

وَتَوَلَّى ۞ أَلَمْ يَعْلَم بِأَنَّ اللَّهَ يَرَى ۞ كَلَّا لَئِن لَّمْ يَنتَهِ لَنَسْفَعًا بِالنَّاصِيَةِ ۞ نَاصِيَةٍ كَاذِبَةٍ

خَاطِئَةٍ ۞ فَلْيَدْعُ نَادِيَهُ ۞ سَنَدْعُ الزَّبَانِيَةَ ۞ كَلَّا لَا تُطِعْهُ وَاسْجُدْ وَاقْتَرِب ۩

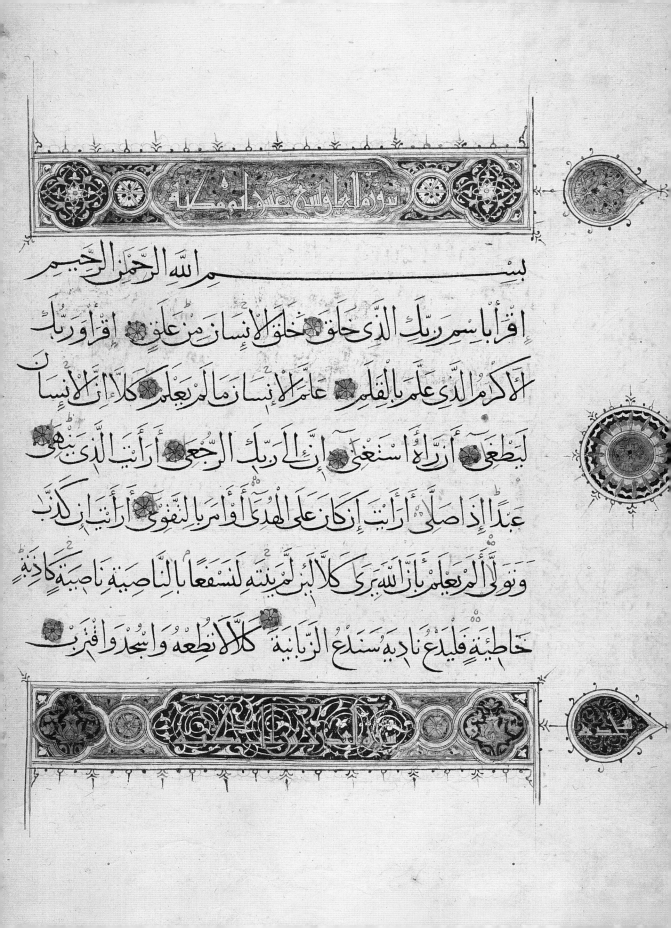

Grand designs

The fourteenth century saw a rise in the number of ornate Qur'ans exhibiting highly developed styles in calligraphy together with a growing confidence in illumination. It should be stressed that whichever aspect of Qur'an manuscripts is being considered – whether calligraphy, ornament or page layout – none can be divorced from the other. Page design is their unifying feature. The development of this artistic form of religious expression was encouraged and flourished under Mamluk and Il-Khanid rule. Between 1250 and 1517, Egypt and most of Syria were governed by the Mamluks, originally non-Muslim slaves in the service of Ayyubid rulers, some of whom became converts to Islam and rose to positions of high office. In Iraq and Persia between 1256 and 1353 political control lay in the hands of the Il-Khanid Mongols who, like the Mamluks, became converts to Islam. Later dynasties between the fourteenth and nineteenth centuries – in particular, the Timurid (1370–1506), Ottoman (1281–1924), Safavid (1501–1732) and Mughal (1526–1858) – saw further developments in the art of ornamentation. Hence over a period of some six hundred years Qur'an manuscript production passed through various stages of grandeur, refinement and sophistication. These qualities are reflected in the ways in which the Qur'an text has been calligraphed and ornamented on the page.

18 OPPOSITE A text page from a 14th-century Mamluk Qur'an, Cairo, written in *muhaqqaq* script with chapter headings in an ornamental eastern *kufic*. The text here contains the whole of chapter ninety-six. According to Muslim tradition, the first five verses of this chapter contain the first revelation that the Prophet Muhammad received.
BL Or.1009, f. 303v.

19 The endowment document of a 14th-century Qur'an, part seven of a set originally in thirty volumes. The document states that this Qur'an was donated by the Amir, Aytmish al-Bajasi, for the library of his mosque in the *Bab al-Wazir*, Cairo. The wording of the document is formulaic, with pietistic expressions and glorifying epithets.
BL Or. 9671, f. 1r (enlarged).

Patronage and documentation

What is known of ornate Qur'ans from the Mamluk period and onwards is mainly gleaned through study of the documentation presented within the volumes themselves. The names of those involved in the manuscript's production – the scribe and illuminator, who were sometimes the same person – are usually found on the colophon at the end of the Qur'an. Here, too, is often noted the date when the copying of the text was completed, together with the name of the city in which the work was carried out. Often, too, is included a page documenting the name of the person who commissioned the Qur'an. Because of its lavish and costly production, an ornate copy required the financial resources of a patron – usually a ruling sultan or an influential member of the court – who donated it as a gift to a mosque or other religious institution (fig. 19). The influence of a patron is immediately discernible in the splendour, grandeur and magnificence of such opulent volumes, as exemplified by the extensive use of gold and other rich colours adorning the text and the design of the decorative pages. In these Qur'ans the architecture of the page layout is enhanced with a sense of space, achieved not necessarily by the physical size of the volume, but by generous margins and the choice of large calligraphic scripts, all of which provide freedom and movement between the lines of text.

The calligrapher and the illuminator

Our knowledge of the art of calligraphy, illumination and the methods used to prepare inks and writing instruments comes mostly from mediaeval sources – from Arabic treatises on the subject, general handbooks and manuals for scribes who, in their capacity as court officials, were responsible for drawing up documents. The calligrapher would be responsible for planning the page for the text, organizing the space of the page and the use of the ruling frame (mistarah) which enabled him to write in straight lines. The calligrapher belonged to a professional class; in order to gain membership to this class, the scribe needed to obtain a diploma (ijazah), after several years of working under a master calligrapher. This apprenticeship, as might be expected, included training in trimming reeds for the pen (quills were not used as in Western Europe) and in the preparation of inks including, among other ingredients, carbon, irongall and gum-arabic. In addition to gold, the palette for the illumination was made up mainly of yellow (orpiment, i.e. yellow arsenic sulphide), white (lead white), orange (red lead or a mixture of red lead and orpiment), blue (lapis lazuli or azurite), red (vermillion or red lead) and green (copper carbonate or a mixture of indigo blue and orpiment).

The task of embellishing the Qur'an would be undertaken by the illuminator on completion of the entire text or, as was often the case in multi-volume Qur'ans, after the completion of a section or a number of sections. It was not uncommon for the illuminator and the calligrapher to have been the same person. Where they were not, it can be assumed that they worked together as a team, collaborating in the planning of the page layout and the format of the volume. It was often the case that a number of illuminators worked together in the same workshop along with the master illuminator, where each artist had a delegated role or responsibility for a complete volume of a multi-volume set. The penmanship of master calligraphers and the artistry of some of the most talented illuminators combined to place these richly produced Qur'ans among the world's most sublime expressions of religious art.

Sultan Baybars' Qur'an

Illustrative of the combination of ornate art and religious feeling is the Baybars Qur'an, so named after its patron, Rukn al-Din Baybars al-Jashnagir, who commissioned it. This Qur'an is the earliest dated Qur'an of the Mamluk period and was produced in seven volumes in Cairo during the years 1304 and 1306. During this time Rukn al-Din Baybars was not yet a sultan but a high chamberlain in the court of al-Nasir Muhammad. Only later, between 1309 and 1310, did he acquire the title of al-Muzaffar Baybars, or Sultan Baybars II. Though Arabic historical sources make reference to his Qur'an, the purpose of his patronage is unclear. It is not known whether the Qur'an was intended as a pious gift to the mosque of al-Hakim in Cairo (built 990–1013), or whether it was intended to be a donation to the building of a religious foundation.

The Baybars Qur'an presents the sacred text in seven volumes, each containing a seventh (*sub*ʿ) of the Qur'an text – a rare arrangement as noted above – and each with its own colophon page (*fig. 20*). With almost as much attention given to its document pages as to the text pages of the Qur'an itself, the colophon is here presented within a cloud-like motif on a pink foliate ground, bordered on all four sides by gold filigree strapwork on a blue ground. We know much about the production of this Qur'an since the attributions on the colophon pages are clear. Both the patron, Rukn al-Din Baybars, and the calligrapher, Muhammad ibn al-Wahid, are mentioned in all the colophons. Ibn al-Wahid was born in Damascus in the mid-thirteenth century though he lived most of his life in Cairo. This Qur'an is the only surviving example of his work. The colophon of the seventh and final volume confirms the date, stating that this Qur'an was completed in its entirety in the year 705 of the Muslim calendar, corresponding to the years 1305–06. We also learn that the master illuminator in charge of a small team was Abu Bakr Sandal, as his signature appears in the colophon page of the third volume within a marginal ornament (*fig. 21*). Although other examples of Sandal's work are known, very little is known about him or his life. The two other members of his team, also documented in this Qur'an, were Muhammad ibn Mubadir and Aydughdi ibn ʿAbdallah al-Badri, about neither of whom is much known.

Each volume of the Baybars Qur'an has a magnificent double frontispiece; these carpet pages are illuminated in the Mamluk style, characterized by the extensive use of geometric patterns and gold filigree work. However, where in earlier Qur'ans the design of these pages is mainly without text of any kind, the Baybars Qur'an introduces into its carpet pages quotations from the Qur'an and, because of its multi-volume presentation, the specific number of the particular volume. To a certain extent, the introduction of inscriptions dictated the

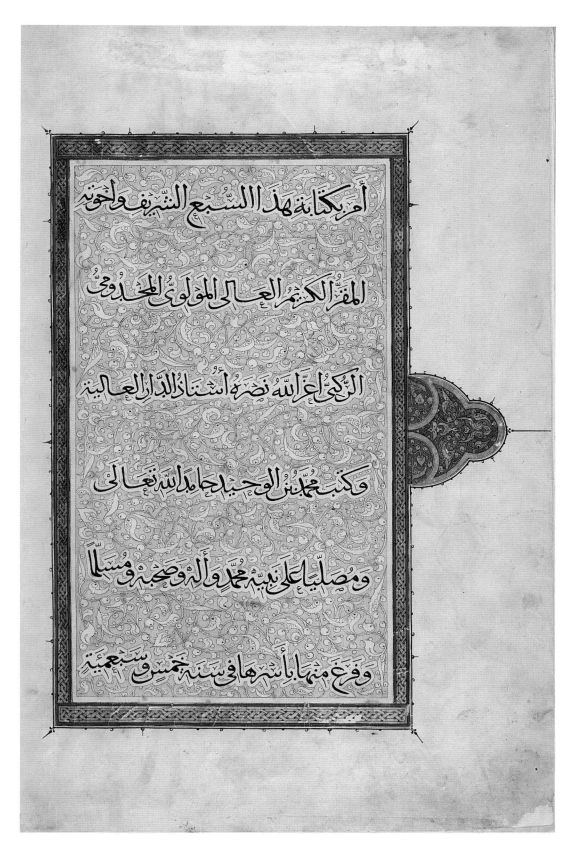

أمر بكتابة هذا السبع الشريف ولخونه

المقر الكريم العالي المولوي المخدومي

الزكي اعز الله نصره أستاذ الدار العالية

وكتبه محمد بن الوحيد حامد الله تعالى

ومصليا على نبيه محمد وآله وصحبه ومسلما

وفرغ منها بأسرها في سنة خمس وسبعمية

21 Detail from the colophon
page of volume three of Sultan
Baybars' Qur'an, 1305–06, with
the signature of the master
illuminator, Abu Bakr Sandal,
inscribed in the ornamental
semi-circles (right).
BL Add.22408, f. 154v.

design of the carpet page. Hence, the rectangular frame, with its division into central and outer panels, can be seen as a suitable structure for combining abstract design with calligraphic text. The double frontispiece of volume three illustrates this point: each of its two central panels is designed in the form of a polygon and carries a word from the title in white *thuluth* script (*fig. 22*). Taken together, these two words give the number of the volume; in this case 'the third seventh'. The four panels, two above and two below the central polygons, quote from chapter four, verse 113 of the Qur'an, which reads 'In the name of God, the Merciful, the Compassionate. God has sent down to you the Book and Wisdom and has taught you what you did not know, and great is God's grace on you'. With the introduction of text into carpet pages, it is clear that each page is dependent on the other; though symmetrical in design, the sense of the text is only complete when the pages are viewed as a whole.

The opening text pages of the Baybars Qur'an – the incipit pages – are somewhat unconventional in their layout (*fig. 23*). Containing the whole of chapter one of the Qur'an (*Surat al-fatihah*), the text is unusually spread over both pages of the opening, written in gold *thuluth* script within a flowing cloud-like motif set against a dotted geometric pattern. Here, the rectangular panels above and below the text are embellished with red and gold motifs on a blue ground, while the whole design is encased in gold with an ornamental clasp projecting into the outer margin of the page.

In contrast, many fourteenth-century Mamluk Qur'ans from Egypt have a more conventional presentation for the whole of chapter one, with the entire chapter set on the first page of the opening, and with the beginning of chapter two (*Surat al-baqarah*) on the second page (*fig.* 24). Another conventional feature of the opening text pages of Mamluk Qur'ans is the tripartite division of the page into a central text panel with upper and lower panels for chapter headings. Unlike the Baybars Qur'an, the upper panels often contain the chapter headings, while the lower panels state the number of verses in the chapter. The inscriptions often reverted to an archaic monumental script such as eastern *kufic*.

While the text of the opening pages in Mamluk Qur'ans was usually presented within a rectangular frame or border, this feature does not necessarily appear on all the other pages of the text. Instead, as seen in the Baybars Qur'an, the illusion of a border is created by wide margins and the alignment of the text (*fig.* 25). The physical size of the Baybars Qur'an enabled the calligrapher and illuminators to work not only with a large script and extensive decoration but also within a spacious page layout. Its 1,094 folios spread over seven volumes, each volume measuring 47.5 x 32 cm, give an indication of its monumental stature.

The splendour of the Baybars Qur'an is further enhanced by being written entirely in gold and in *thuluth* script. This cursive hand is here outlined in black ink, with vowels marked in red and other spelling signs in blue. The choice of *thuluth* as the script is also strange, for this script was generally considered ornamental, being used primarily for chapter headings and not for the body of the text. It would appear that *thuluth* had assumed to a great extent the same role as *kufic* and eastern *kufic* scripts during the Mamluk period, when they were mainly used for Qur'anic quotations in carpet pages or illuminated chapter headings. The layout of the calligraphy is also of special interest as each page of the Baybars Qur'an carries an even number of lines. This is virtually without precedence, for most Qur'ans with few exceptions have an odd number of lines per page. Of interest, too, is the fact that the text layout is continuous, without large illuminated rectangular panels to indicate the beginning of a chapter, as in many other Qur'ans of this period. In the Baybars Qur'an, chapter headings

22 The carpet pages designed by Abu Bakr Sandal, from
volume three of Sultan Baybars' Qur'an. BL Add.22408, ff. IV-2.

23 The incipit pages of Sultan Baybars' Qur'an containing
the whole of chapter one. BL Add.22406, ff. 3v-4.

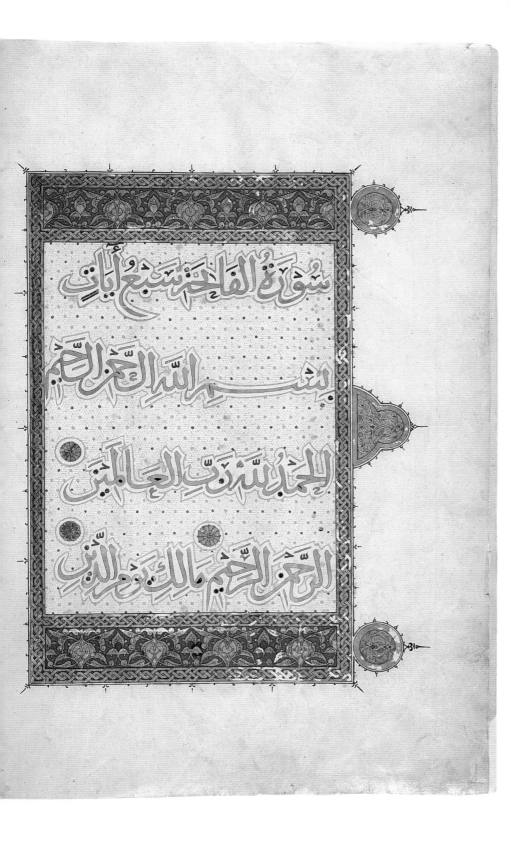

24 By contrast with Sultan Baybars' Qur'an, compare this typical design
for incipit pages from a 14th-century Mamluk Qur'an, Cairo, with chapter
headings and number of verses in the upper and lower panels. BL Or.1009, ff. 2v-3.

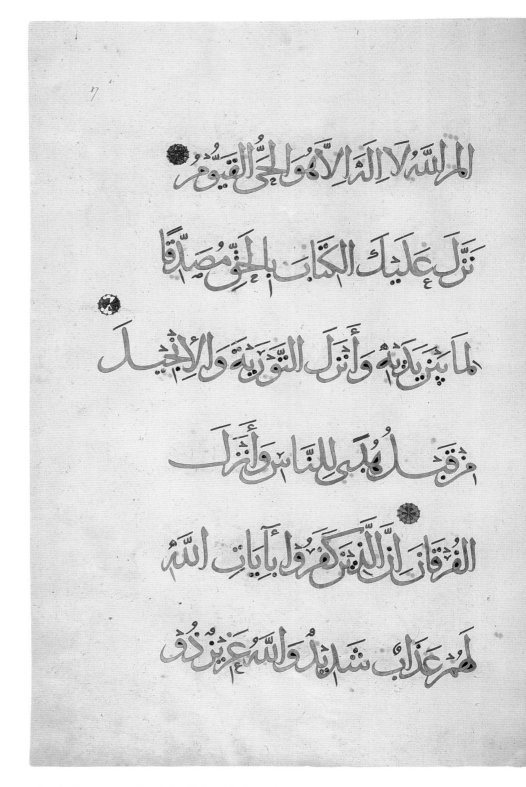

الۤمۤ ۞ اللهُ لَاۤ اِلٰهَ اِلَّاۤ هُوَ الْحَيُّ الْقَيُّومُ

نَزَّلَ عَلَيْكَ الْكِتَابَ بِالْحَقِّ مُصَدِّقًا

لِمَا بَيْنَ يَدَيْهِ وَاَنْزَلَ التَّوْرٰىةَ وَالْاِنْجِيلَ

مِنْ قَبْلُ هُدًى لِلنَّاسِ وَاَنْزَلَ

الْفُرْقَانَ اِنَّ الَّذِينَ كَفَرُوا بِاٰيَاتِ اللهِ

لَهُمْ عَذَابٌ شَدِيدٌ وَاللهُ عَزِيزٌ ذُو

25 Continuing text pages from Sultan Baybars' Qur'an, written
in gold *thuluth* script outlined in black. Vowels are marked in red,
and other spelling signs in blue. BL Add.22406, ff. 86v-87.

عَلَيْنَا إِصْرًا كَمَا حَمَلْتَهُ عَلَى الَّذِينَ

قَبْلِنَا رَبَّنَا وَلَا تُحَمِّلْنَا مَا لَا طَاقَةَ لَنَا

بِهِ وَاعْفُ عَنَّا وَاغْفِرْ لَنَا وَارْحَمْنَا أَنْتَ

مَوْلَانَا فَانْصُرْنَا عَلَى الْقَوْمِ الْكَافِرِينَ

سُورَةُ آلِ عِمْرَانَ مِائَتَا آيَةٍ مَكِّيَّةٌ

بِسْمِ اللَّهِ الرَّحْمَنِ الرَّحِيمِ

are merely indicated by a change of colour, with red ink overlaying the gold, but with no additional spacing between the lines. It would seem that the calligrapher viewed the text of the Qur'an as a complete entity and did not wish to interrupt the visual flow of the page (figs. 26, 27, 28).

A Royal Qur'an from Iraq

Individuality in the copying and illumination of Qur'ans is also found, not only in the Baybars Qur'an but in other ornate Qur'ans of this period, such as the one commissioned five years later in Mosul (Iraq) by the Il-Khanid ruler, Uljaytu (r. 1304–17). In many respects the differences between these two Qur'ans are striking, making it hard to appreciate that they belong to the same period, but perhaps this is due to the fact that they come from different regions. Variety and style of presentation can be seen in the range of motifs used in the design of the decorated pages of the multi-volume Uljaytu Qur'an. Many of these were inspired by the structure of the mosque. The influence of this architecture is particularly evident in the colophon page of volume twenty-five, where the rectangular frame, containing the text, is shaped in the form of a prayer-niche (mihrab) (fig. 29). This colophon states that the scribe of this volume, and of all preceding volumes, is 'Ali ibn Muhammad al-Husayni, and that this Qur'an was completed in Mosul in the year 710 of the Muslim calendar (corresponding to the year 1310).

The commissioning certificate of the same Qur'an also provides a more elaborate version of the prayer-niche motif within its rectangular framework (fig. 30). The text is written between ruled lines, giving the page the effect of a mistarah, which is the ruling frame that scribes used for writing on paper. The certificate identifies the patron as Sultan Ulyajtu, and traces his ancestry back to Genghis Khan. The names of two of the Sultan's viziers, Sa'd al-Din and Rashid al-Din, are also mentioned.

The carpet pages of this Qur'an of the Il-Khanid period show a completely different approach to design from that of the Baybars Qur'an and others normally associated with the Mamluk period (fig. 31). The carpet pages are not compartmentalized into sections, but constructed as a complete visual unit, with the main part of the illumination taken up by the whole rectangle; hence there is no room, nor could there be any intention, for the inclusion of Qur'anic inscriptions. This design, though remarkable for its execution of Mongol-style

26 TOP Detail of an illuminated oval marker from Sultan Baybars' Qur'an. The marker contains the word 'prostration' (*sajdah*) to instruct the reader when to prostrate during the recitation of the Qur'an. BL Add. 22412, f. 156r (detail, enlarged).

27 ABOVE Detail of an illuminated medallion from Sultan Baybars' Qur'an. The Arabic for 'ten' ('*ashr*) in gold *kufic* script indicates the end of a tenth verse. BL 22409, f. 92r (detail, enlarged).

28 RIGHT Detail of an illuminated pear-shaped medallion from Sultan Baybars' Qur'an. The Arabic for 'five' (*khams*) in gold *kufic* script indicates the end of a fifth verse. BL 22412, f. 156v (detail, enlarged).

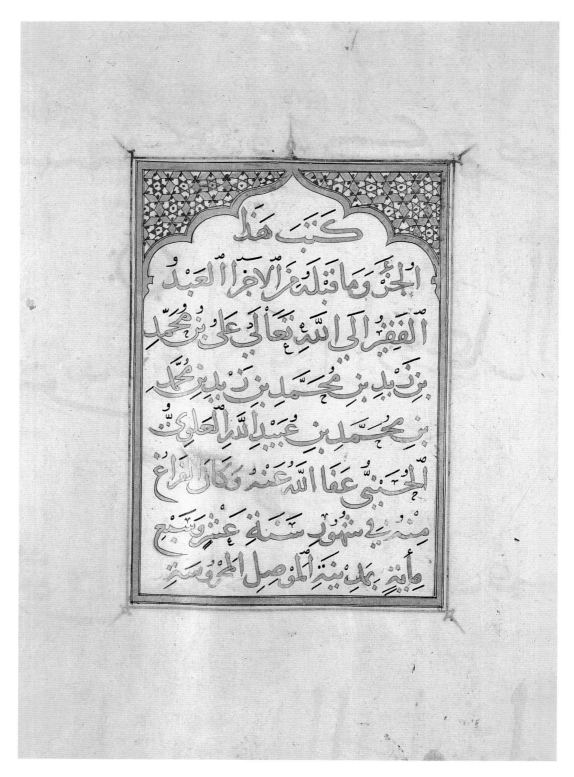

كتب هذا

الجزء وما قبله من الاجزاء العبد

الفقير الى الله تعالى علي بن محمد

بن يزيد بن محمد بن يزيد بن محمد

بن محمد بن عبيد الله العلوي

الحسني عفا الله عنه وكان الفراغ

منه في شهور سنة عشر وسبع

مائة بمدينة الموصل المحروسة

29 The colophon page of volume twenty-five of a Qur'an in thirty volumes,
commissioned for the Il-Khanid ruler, Uljaytu, in Mosul. The full name
of the scribe, 'Ali ibn Muhammad al-Husayni, is noted, and also its date
of completion 710 [1310] and place of origin. BL Or.4945, f. 51v.

30 The commissioning certificate of volume twenty-five of the Uljaytu Qur'an, documenting the name of its patron, the Sultan Uljaytu. BL Or.4945, f. 1r.

31 The carpet pages from volume twenty-five of the Uljaytu Qur'an, remarkable for
their Mongol style of illumination and exquisite colouring. BL Or.4945, ff. 1v-2.

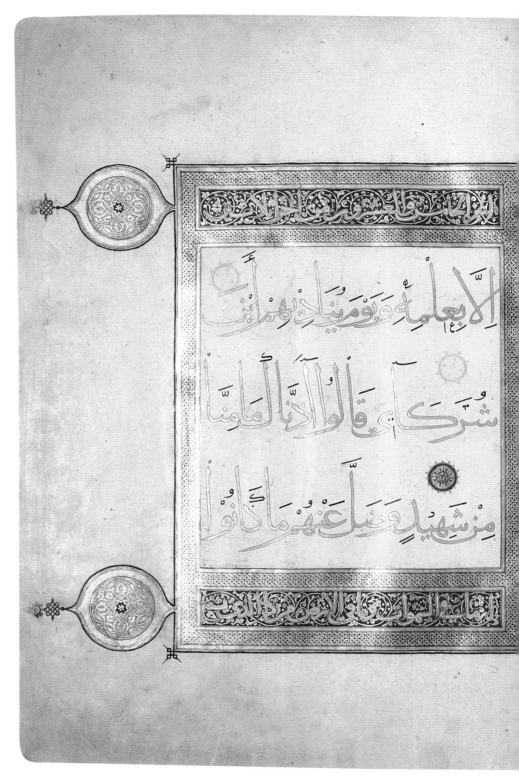

32 The incipit pages from volume twenty-five of the Uljaytu Qur'an, written in gold *muhaqqaq* script. with vowel signs in black. The lower panels contain part of the 'Throne Verse' (chapter 2, verse 255). BL Or.4945, ff. 2v-3.

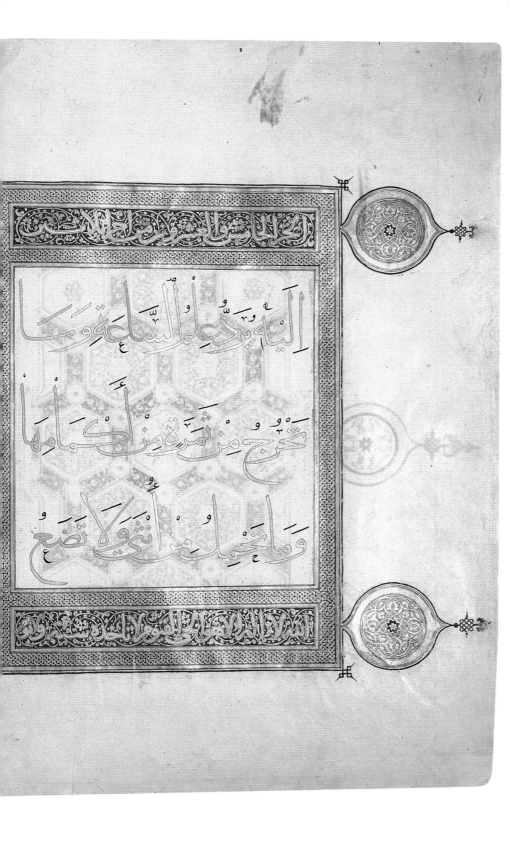

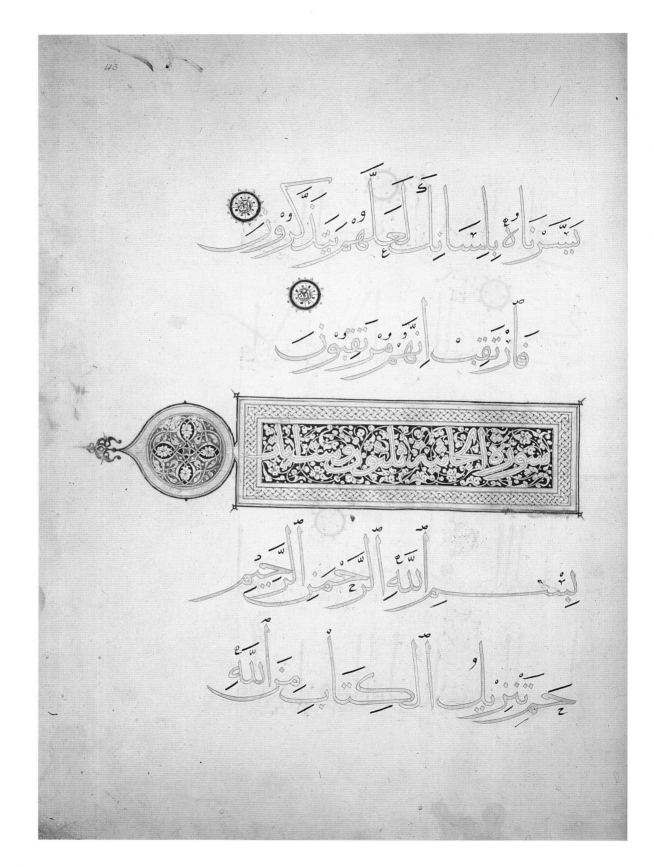

بِسَنَاهُ بِلِسَانِكَ لَعَلَّهُمْ يَتَذَكَّرُونَ

فَارْتَقِبْ اِنَّهُمْ مُرْتَقِبُونَ

سُورَةُ الجاثية مائة وسِتّ آياتٌ

بِسْمِ اللهِ الرَّحْمٰنِ الرَّحِيمِ

حم تَنْزِيلُ الْكِتَابِ مِنَ اللهِ

illumination, is nevertheless conventional. This is exemplified by the extensive use of geometric patterns, the basic features of which are interlocking hexagons decorated with gold arabesques alternating on a red or blue ground. The hexagons are made even more complex by having at their centre a smaller hexagon, each with a gold floral design, also alternating on a red or blue ground. Conventionally too, the whole interconnecting framework is highlighted in white, thus forming smaller hexagons at each intersection.

The opening pages of this Qur'an contain the text in a central panel within a rectangular frame, written in gold *muhaqqaq* script with vowel signs in black ink (*fig. 32*). This was a popular script for larger Qur'ans of the Mamluk and Il-Khanid periods, its angular and cursive features – unlike the *thuluth* of the Baybars Qur'an – giving the calligrapher an opportunity to combine fluidity with rigidity. Again, the conventional use of panelling to carry inscriptions is integral to the rectangular frame surrounding the text, as is the decorative palmette extending from the upper and lower panels into the margin. The inscription records that this section is volume twenty-five of a thirty-volume Qur'an. It is one of the few complete parts of this multi-volume set to have survived intact. Like the Baybars Qur'an, the text pages following the incipit opening are unframed but, unlike the Baybars Qur'an, the Uljaytu does not have an even number of lines; it follows the more usual practice of having an odd number per page (*fig. 33*). The ornamental chapter heading written within a rectangular panel also does not depart from conventional practice, nor does the use of *kufic* script for the roundels which mark the end of each verse, each with the Arabic word for 'verse' (*ayah*) inscribed at its centre.

The Mamluk Qur'an of Sultan Barquq

An outstanding example of a manuscript whose design illustrates the balance between function, ornament, script and layout, is the fourteenth-century Qur'an donated to a mosque in Cairo by the Mamluk Sultan, Faraj ibn Barquq, who reigned during the period 1399–1412 (*fig. 34*). The religious inspiration of a mosque is immediately evident from the gold architectural structure containing the word 'prostration' (*sajdah*) in blue *kufic*. This feature is not only ornamental but has a liturgical purpose, instructing the believer when to prostrate during the recitation of the Qur'an. On the opposite page, balancing the mosque-inspired structure, is an almond-shaped ornament which, again, is

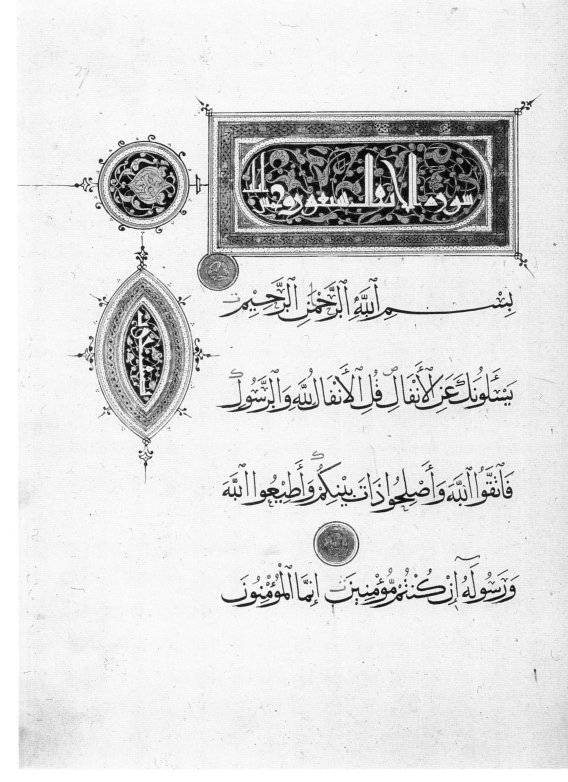

بِسْمِ ٱللَّهِ ٱلرَّحْمَٰنِ ٱلرَّحِيمِ

يَسْـَٔلُونَكَ عَنِ ٱلْأَنفَالِ قُلِ ٱلْأَنفَالُ لِلَّهِ وَٱلرَّسُولِ

فَٱتَّقُوا۟ ٱللَّهَ وَأَصْلِحُوا۟ ذَاتَ بَيْنِكُمْ وَأَطِيعُوا۟ ٱللَّهَ

وَرَسُولَهُۥٓ إِن كُنتُم مُّؤْمِنِينَ إِنَّمَا ٱلْمُؤْمِنُونَ

34 Ornate text pages written in *rayhani* script from the 14th-century Mamluk
Qur'an of Sultan Faraj ibn Barquq, Cairo. BL Or.848, ff. 26v-27.

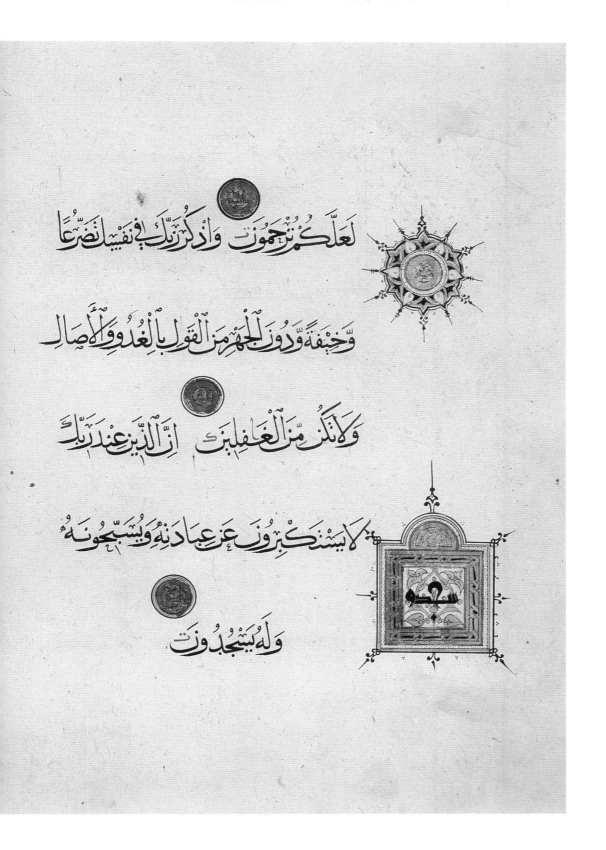

لَعَلَّكُمْ تُرْحَمُونَ ۝ وَاذْكُر رَّبَّكَ فِى نَفْسِكَ تَضَرُّعًا

وَخِيفَةً وَدُونَ الْجَهْرِ مِنَ الْقَوْلِ بِالْغُدُوِّ وَالْآصَالِ

وَلَا تَكُن مِّنَ الْغَافِلِينَ ۝ إِنَّ الَّذِينَ عِندَ رَبِّكَ

لَا يَسْتَكْبِرُونَ عَنْ عِبَادَتِهِ وَيُسَبِّحُونَهُ

وَلَهُ يَسْجُدُونَ ۩

35 The incipit page (left) and carpet page (right) from part nine of
Sultan Faraj ibn Barquq's thirty-volume Qur'an. BL Or.848, ff. IV-2.

36 The incipit pages from an early Ottoman Qur'an of the 15th century, containing the text of the whole of chapter one and the first three verses of chapter two.
BL Or.4810, ff. IV-2.

functional: it marks the beginning of one half of the sixty parts into which the Qur'an text is divided, and hence contains the words 'half a sixtieth' (*nisf hizb*) in white *kufic*. The chapter heading within the rectangular panel is also in white *kufic*. This monumental angular script contrasts magnificently with the refined cursive black *rayhani* script used for the body of the text, while the layout of the unframed lines combines with the calligraphy to give an impression of infinite space.

Although this Qur'an was designed in thirty parts, its carpet pages and incipit pages have only partially survived (fig. 35). The first opening of this manuscript now contains only what remains of the double carpet pages and incipit pages, the leaf that originally lay between them having been lost. As in most Mamluk Qur'ans, the frame of the incipit page is divided into three sections, the middle section of which contains the text within a flowing cloud-like motif set against a background of scrolls. The fragments of inscription within the panels of the incipit page suggest that the complete version stated that this volume was part nine of a thirty-volume set, and that the inscription also carried a quotation from chapter 56, verses 77–80. This quotation must have been inscribed on the incipit page, as it is clear that the carpet page was not designed to carry

any inscription whatsoever. The general effect of the carpet page design is that of a rich tapestry, based on a ten-angled star-shaped medallion with gold and white outlines extending to form a trellis of overlapping polygons which alternate in gold and blue.

37 Shamsah medallions from a 16th-century Qur'an, Afghanistan or possibly India. BL Or.11544, ff. 2v-3.

Developments in style: shamsah medallion, carpet and prayer pages

Under Timurid patronage in the fifteenth century, a new delicacy and refinement began to replace the Il-Khanid style of illumination in Persia and Iraq. This development also spread to Turkey, where the Qur'ans produced under the early Ottomans, though often smaller in scale, were no less impressive than the huge monumental Qur'ans of the Il-Khanid and Mamluk periods (fig. 36). The decorated incipit pages are typical of an exquisite and refined design, which nevertheless still retains many of the features associated with Qur'ans of the preceding century. The cloud-chain motif surrounding the text continues to dominate the central compartment of the frame. Equally conventional are the rectangular panels in gold strapwork, in which the upper panels contain the chapter headings, while the lower panels contain the number of verses in the chapters.

38 The incipit pages of a 16th-century Qur'an, Afghanistan or possibly India.
BL Or.11544, ff. 3v-4

By the time the Safavid dynasty came to rule in Iran – between 1501 and 1732 – the use of carpet pages as frontispieces was almost phased out. As seen in a sixteenth-century Qur'an from Afghanistan (or possibly India), these carpet pages were replaced by a large sunburst in the form of a medallion, often presented within a star-shaped design. The name of this medallion in Arabic is *shamsah* ('sun'), so-called because its shape and illumination resemble the sun and its brightness (fig. 37). The central position of the *shamsah* on the page no doubt contributes to the visual intensity of the illumination, its burst of light contrasting with the rest of the blank page. The medallions, although normally plain without any text, sometimes contained Qur'anic inscriptions. Just as some double carpet pages contain interrelated inscriptions, so pages with inscribed *shamsah* medallions depend on each other for their meaning, and can only be understood when seen as a whole.

Since the *shamsah* medallion replaced the carpet page as a frontispiece, it was only natural for the carpet page itself to develop a new role. Consequently, the carpet page is now incorporated in the same sixteenth-century Qur'an as part of the decorated incipit pages of text (figs. 2 and 38). In this new function, the carpet page contains within its design not merely Qur'anic inscriptions,

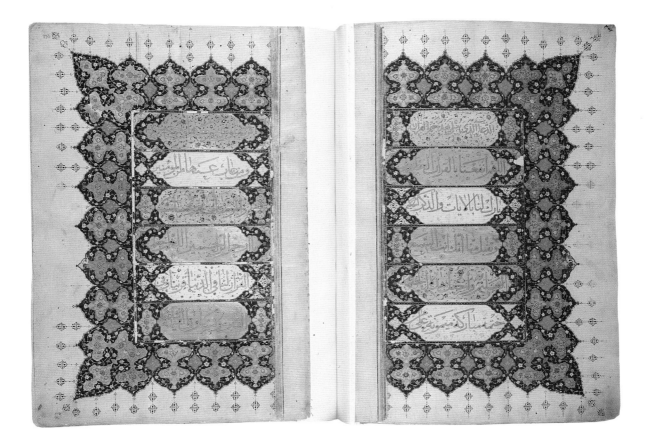

but a whole body of text. In the case of this Qur'an, the two incipit pages carry the whole of chapter one (*Surat al-fatihah*), together with the chapter heading and a statement of the number of verses in the chapter. Where the carpet pages of other Qur'ans are compartmentalized, with the result that their inscriptions appear constrained, here, by contrast, the general effect is one of freedom, since the whole of the text, presented at the focal point of each page, merges naturally with its ultramarine background and the surrounding shapes. The symmetry of layout and design – gold palmettes and scrollwork around three sides of a rectangle with blue tassels protruding into the margin, and smaller palmettes alternating in blue and pink – all contribute to the visual unity of these incipit pages.

It is customary for Muslims to recite a special prayer on completing a reading of the whole Qur'an (*fig. 39*). These extra pages, which contain the concluding prayer at the end of the volume, are sometimes highly decorative. In the same sixteenth-century Qur'an, for example, the prayer pages have the same format as a carpet page, with each line of text on the right-hand page in gold set against an alternating background of blue, pink and yellow cartouches. For theological and doctrinal reasons – since only God is perfect – the symmetry of design in the decorative pages of Qur'ans is not exact. Usually the symmetry is

39 The prayer pages from a 16th-century Qur'an with alternating coloured cartouches, Afghanistan or possibly India. BL Or.11544, ff. 372v-373.

40 OPPOSITE A Qur'an from Herat in Afghanistan, dated 970/1563, with text in a variety of scripts. See below examples of a chapter heading (bottom right) and marginal ornaments (bottom left). BL Or.13087, ff. 83v-84 (details enlarged).

subtly broken; in this case, however, the asymmetry is obvious. For, though the cartouches on both pages are in the same colours, the left-hand page presents them in a different order.

New layouts for text

In the Qur'ans we have so far examined, the text pages – with the exception of decorated incipit pages – can be considered as a visual unit. However, this is not necessarily the case in the text pages of Qur'ans produced during the Safavid, Mughal and Ottoman periods. Typically, the area allotted for the text is partitioned within a rectangular framework, thus enabling a number of scripts to be used on the same page. There is no doubt that this format allowed the scribe to display his skills in a number of styles for the sake of variety and emphasis, as well as for making the page more decorative. An illustration of this is the design for a text page in a sixteenth-century Qur'an from Herat in Afghanistan, where the calligrapher has used four different styles of Arabic script (fig. 40). The first, middle and last lines within the overall framework are in gold *thuluth* script; the remaining lines in the two larger compartments are in black *naskhi*; while white *ruq'ah* script is employed for the chapter heading within the horizontal panel. Following convention, as we have already seen in previous Qur'ans, *kufic* is the preferred script in the ornamental directions for reading the text. It should be noted that the positioning of the rectangular framework provides wide margins for these inscribed ornaments, which in the form of medallions join up to form a functional verse counter. The word *sajdah* ('prostration') within the pear-shaped medallion is functionally placed close to the chapter heading to remind the worshipper that it is necessary to prostrate at this point in the reading, while the oval-shaped ornament containing the word *hizb* in *kufic* script indicates the beginning of a sixtieth section of the text.

In Qur'ans where the text is constrained within a rectangular framework, or in those Qur'ans where the framework encasing the text is divided into sections, the middle opening of the volume is often given a more elaborate treatment, much in the same way as that given to their decorated opening pages. Hence, the centre text pages of a sixteenth-century Qur'an from India have a carpet page design (fig. 41). The text here is split up, with alternating scripts in different coloured inks. The first, middle and last lines are written in an alternating gold and blue *muhaqqaq* script on a white ground, while the two main

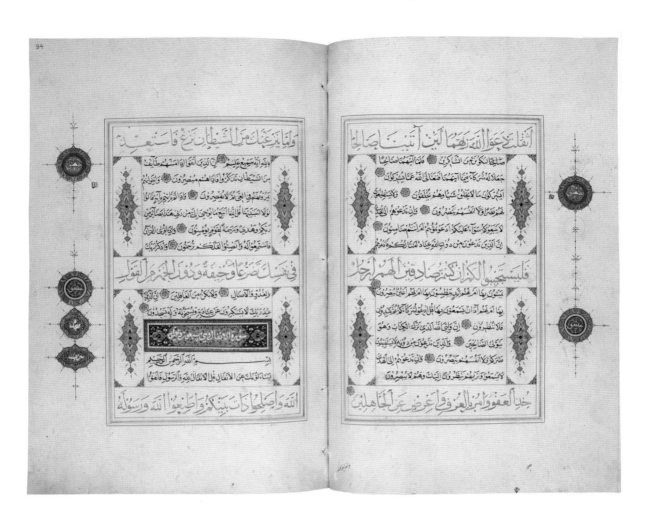

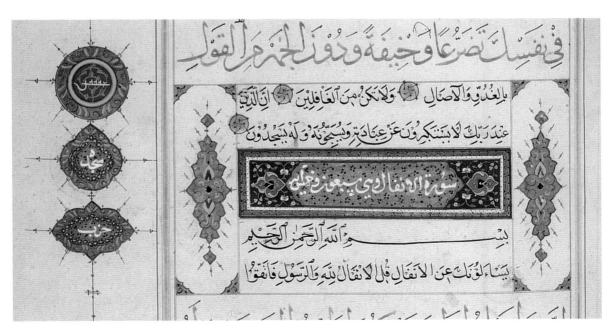

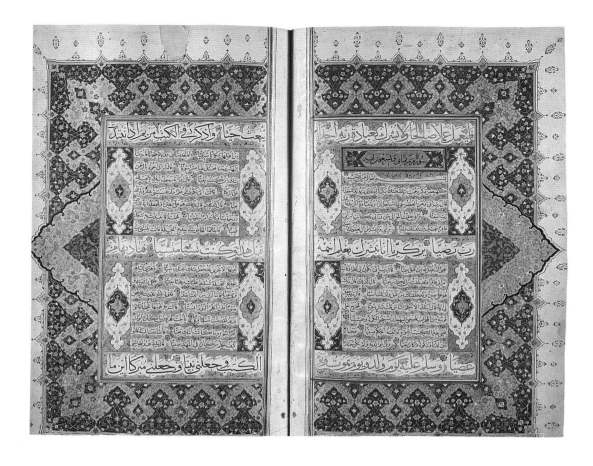

41 The central text pages from a 16th-century Qur'an, India, with a carpet page design. BL Add.18497, ff. 118v-119.

panels of text are in black *naskhi* on a gold ground with red and blue flowers. In this Qur'an, the use of different scripts penned in various colours is purely for decoration and variety. They do not draw attention to particular words or phrases since the text on the page reads as one continuous piece.

Scripts and their function

Scripts in various styles and colours, however, were employed not only for decorative purposes. They often had a more functional role, highlighting specific words or sentences. This was to help the reader to identify the hierarchy of texts where more than one text appeared on the page; and it was particularly important for those pages which carry not only the sacred text but also a translation of the original Arabic. An example of this is demonstrated in a Qur'an from India, copied around 1500 during the rule of the Delhi sultans (fig. 42). The text, in black ink, is in a variety of *naskhi* script known as *bihari*, so named after the province of Bihar in northern India with which this style of script became associated. The Persian translation is written between the lines and is penned in red *naskhi* in a minute hand, so as not to diminish the status of the sacred text. Emphasis is given to the word *Allah* (God), the name being highlighted in blue

throughout the text, and in gold where the name is mentioned in the pious invocation (*basmalah*) beneath the illuminated chapter heading. Deference to the divine name is given by penning the name of God in another colour; this appears to be a common feature of Qur'ans in *bihari* script. According to Islamic tradition the Qur'an is inimitable in any language, so the interlinear translations at their very best were no more than aids to comprehension.

A seventeenth-century Qur'an from Persia solved the same problem of accommodating the Qur'an text together with its translation on the same page by adopting a different approach to its presentation (*fig. 43*). While using different scripts and coloured inks to differentiate between the original Arabic text and its translation, the two texts are here presented together within a rectangular structure which resembles the ruling frame (*mistarah*) used by scribes for ruling lines on paper. The Qur'an text in black *naskhi* script alternates with its interlinear Persian translation written in a small red *nasta'liq* – a Persian script developed in the late fifteenth century. Like the sixteenth-century Qur'an from Herat (*fig. 40*), the individual marginal medallions in this Persian Qur'an join up to form a verse counter, the ornamental instructions here being in *thuluth* script rather than in archaic *kufic*. The alternating scripts find their counterpart

42 An early 16th-century Qur'an from India written in *bihari* script. Note the interlinear Persian translation penned in red *naskhi* script.
BL Add.5551, ff. 135v-136.

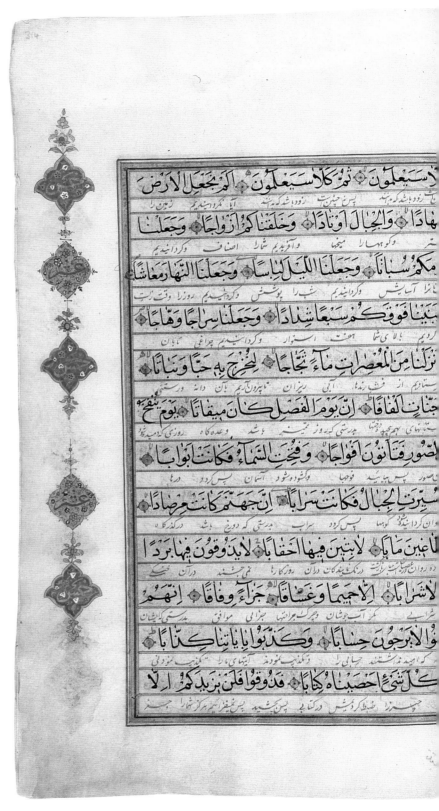

43 A 17th-century Qur'an from Persia written in *naskhi* script, with an interlinear Persian translation in red *nasta'liq* script. BL Or.13371, ff. 313v–314.

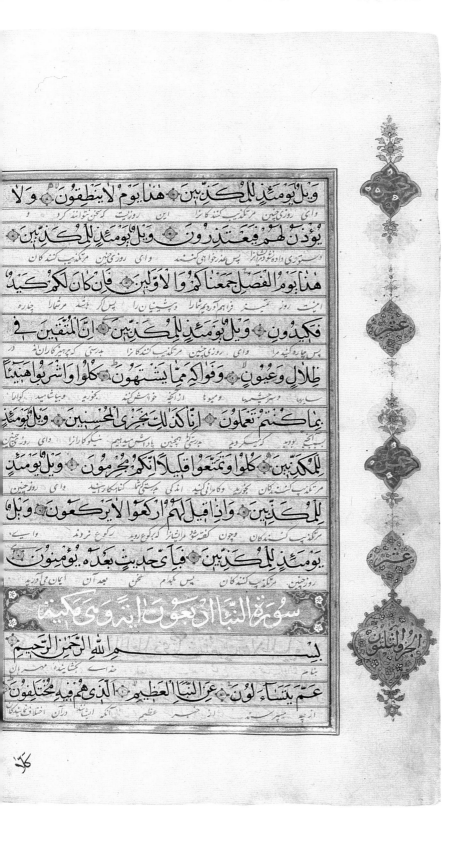

44 A Qur'an from Morocco, dated 975/1568, commissioned by the Sharifi Sultan, 'Abdallah ibn Muhammad. BL Or.1405, ff. 370v-371.

in the marginal ornaments, where the gold on blue of the fifth verse marker contrasts with the blue on gold of the tenth verse marker. The visual unity of the overall design is achieved through a subtle combination of scripts, coloured inks, and the positioning of the marginal ornaments.

The spatial dimension

The distribution of text on the page does not necessarily need to be generous for the layout to create a sense of space and grandeur. As already seen in those Qur'ans from the Islamic East which are written in early *naskhi* script, the compactness of the text area is often a major feature of their page design. To some extent, this spatial effect was determined by the style of script. A high density of text is also characteristic of many Qur'ans produced in the Islamic West, written in *maghribi* script. This is particularly evident in a Qur'an from Morocco, copied in 975/1568 for the Sharifi Sultan, 'Abdallah ibn Muhammad (fig. 44). Here the dynamics operating between the compact text and the illuminated marginal devices work well together due to their proximity, giving the impression of wide margins and spaciousness on the page. The pear-shaped medallions, their gold arabesque designs outlined in blue and picked out in red and

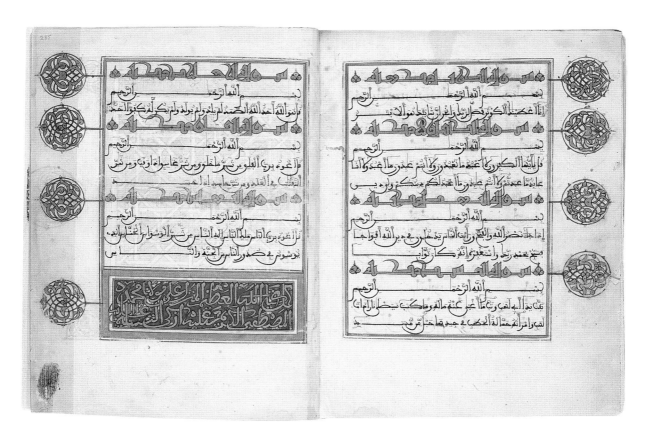

green, contain the word for 'five' (*khams*) in white *kufic* script, each positioned near the line of text which contains the end of a fifth verse. Likewise, the marginal large roundels containing the word for 'ten' (*'ashr*) in white *kufic* script are functionally placed to indicate the end of a tenth verse. An additional feature which adds to compactness is the reinforcement in the text of the fifth and tenth verse counts. The letter *ha'* in gold is inserted to mark the end of a fifth verse, *ha'* having the numerical value of five in the Arabic alphanumeric system. A tenth verse is indicated by the insertion of a gold roundel, while gold knots indicate the end of the other verses. A contrasting use of the same script (*maghribi*) can be seen in an early eighteenth-century Moroccan Qur'an (*fig. 45*). Here, it gives an uncrowded, free-flowing grace to the text despite being encased within a fixed border. Admittedly, the script is elongated and has more space between the lines than in the *maghribi* Qur'an produced some two centuries earlier (*fig. 44*).

45 A Qur'an from Morocco, dated 1113/1701–2, containing the last seven chapters of the Qur'an. Each of the chapter headings is indicated by a palmette in the margin, as is the blue end panel. BL Or.13382, ff. 284v-285.

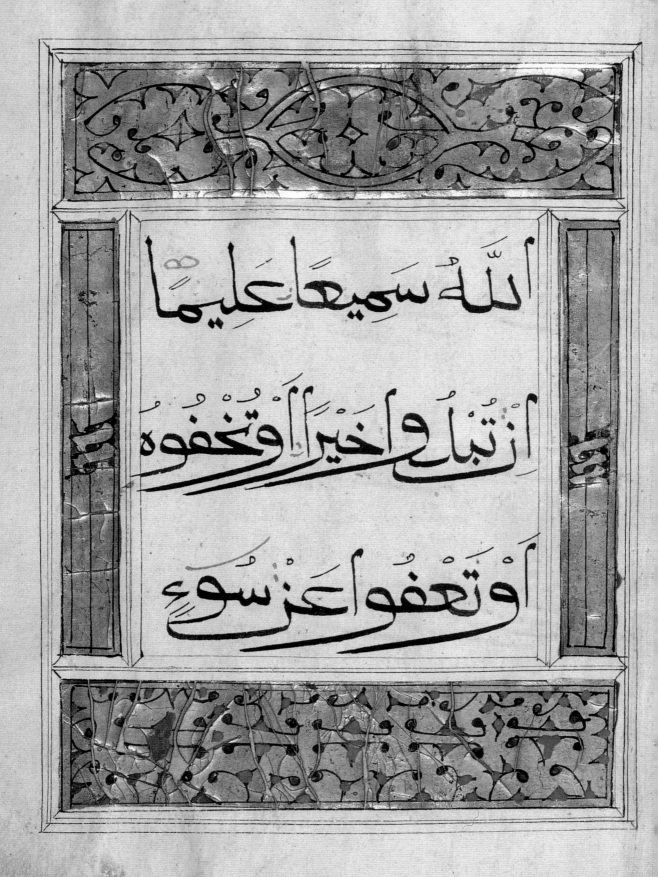

اللَّهَ سَمِيعًا عَلِيمًا

اِنْ تُبْدُوا خَيْرًا اَوْ تُخْفُوهُ

اَوْ تَعْفُوا عَنْ سُوءٍ

Qur'an manuscripts
and the spread of Islam

Due to the economic and cultural impact of Muslim traders and travellers on the countries they visited, Islam gradually spread from the Near and Middle East to regions where it was not the dominant faith. With the advance of Islam into these new areas – South East Asia, China and its border with Central Asia – institutions such as mosques, schools and religious academies (*madrasahs*) were needed to meet the requirements of the new Muslim communities. Because the Qur'an and its teachings are central to the Muslim way of life, religious scholars and teachers consequently left Arabia and the Indian subcontinent to teach in these new areas, while locally trained teachers were sent to study at major institutes in Mecca and Medina and other centres of the Arab world, such as the al-Azhar in Cairo, the world's oldest university. At the same time, the growing need to provide the Muslim communities with copies of the Qur'an for prayer and study made it necessary to train calligraphers drawn from their own communities. This resulted in the assimilation of local traditions in manuscripts produced in areas not normally associated with the art of Islamic calligraphy and illumination. While the illumination and decoration have the same function in all Qur'ans, the influence of local style and culture is manifest, without infringing Islamic practice in sacred art.

46 OPPOSITE A decorative text page from a 17th-century Chinese Qur'an written in *sini* script.
BL Or.15256/1, f.2r (enlarged).

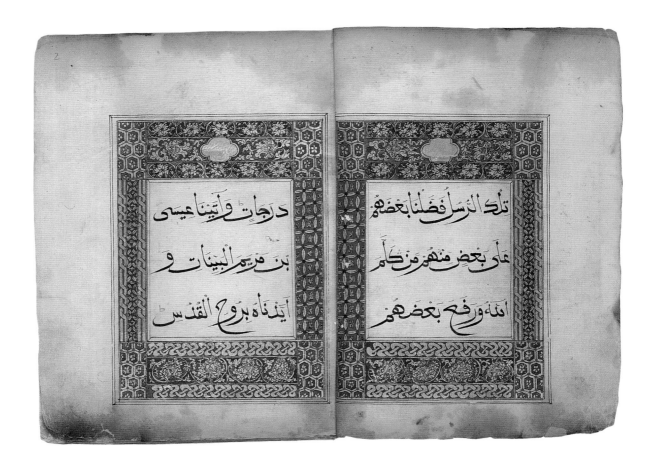

47 The incipit pages of a late 17th-century Chinese Qur'an written in *sini* script. The decorative style is Central Asian. Part three of a set originally in thirty volumes. BL Or.15571, ff. 1v-2.

Qur'ans from China

In the eighth century Muslim merchants were already trading in China. A community is known to have been established in Xian, where a mosque was built in 742. However, the impact of Islam in China and Central Asia was not strongly felt until the period of Mongol rule in the thirteenth century. The network of trade routes from Europe via Samarqand in Central Asia to China was a major factor in this development; this network, known as the Silk Road, became the conduit for the spread of religious and cultural influences as well as for goods and merchandise. In China, as in other parts of the Muslim world, Qur'an manuscript production followed traditional Islamic methods and practice, with the bound volume (codex) as the preferred format; these Chinese Qur'ans were generally produced in thirty-volume sets. The script, a variation of *muhaqqaq*, is penned in a way which suggests that the pen strokes were influenced by Chinese calligraphy, and is often referred to as *sini* ('Chinese') Arabic. A central panel is a prominent feature of Chinese Qur'ans on their decorated pages, which usually contain as few as three lines of text, with only a few words on each (figs. 47 and 48).

Another Chinese influence is evident in the decorated pages – particularly

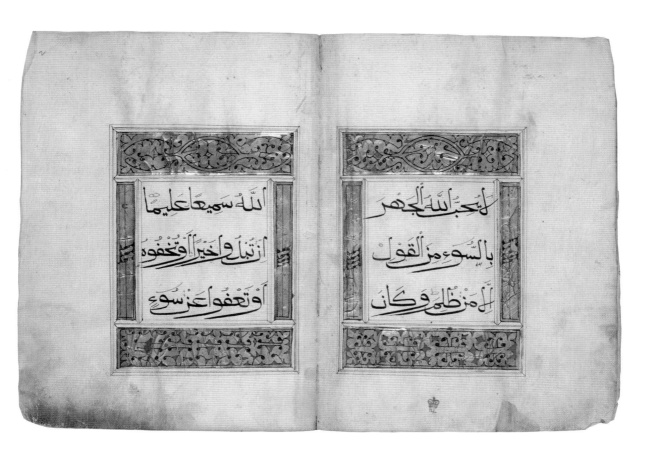

in the page designs of the first and last openings of the text – as seen in a seventeenth-century Qur'an, with its use of vibrant colours or gold for typical motifs such as crescents and banners (fig. 49). Many Chinese Qur'ans incorporate intricate circles in the upper and lower panels of their decorative pages; these can be seen here to overlap, producing half circles alternating in gold and blue. A cluster of red dots on a green and blue ground gives emphasis to the central ovals within the panels. The motif for these panels seems to have been dictated by the *shamsah* (sun burst) illumination which dominates the preceding page of this Qur'an (fig. 50). This is in the form of a large medallion, the central feature of which is an intricate design based on overlapping circles to give the impression of petals. The cluster at the centre of the medallion is replicated by smaller versions in each of the outer circles, while the outer ring of the medallion itself is in gold, which again is surrounded by two outer rings in black. As with other *shamsah* medallions, the whole effect of this Chinese *shamsah* is one of illuminated brilliance. This medallion carries no inscription; however, when Arabic script is used in other Chinese Qur'ans to inscribe text within an ornament, the script often suggests Chinese decoration and imagery. This can be readily appreciated in the calligraphic style of a Qur'anic inscription

48 The incipit pages of a 17th-century Chinese Qur'an written in *sini* script, part six of a set originally in thirty volumes. BL Or.15256/1, ff.1v-2.

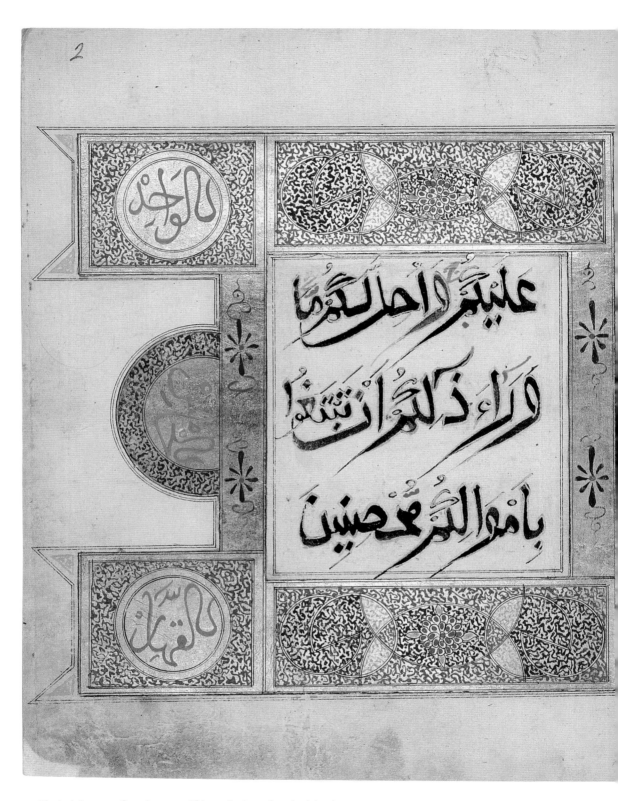

49 The incipit pages of a 17th-century Chinese Qur'an written in sini script, part five of a set originally in thirty volumes. BL Or.15604, ff. 1v-2.

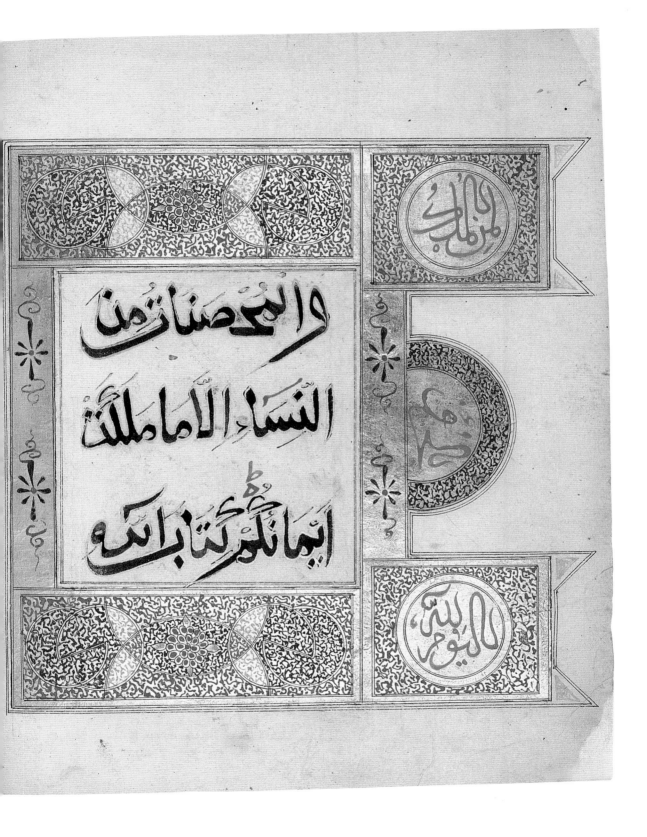

50 A *shamsah* medallion from
a 17th-century Chinese Qur'an.
Note the intricate design of
overlapping circles, creating
the impression of petals.
BL Or.15604, f. 1r (detail, enlarged).

51 A *shamsah* medallion from
an 18th-century Chinese Qur'an,
part ten of a set originally in
thirty volumes. The Qur'anic
inscription states: 'I seek refuge in
Allah from the accursed Satan'.
BL Or.14758, f. 2r (detail, enlarged).

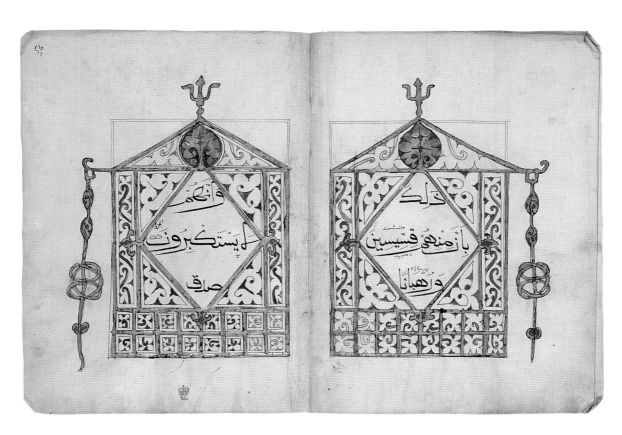

52 ABOVE The decorated final text opening with lantern motif from a 17th-century Chinese Qur'an.
BL Or.15256/1, ff. 55v-56.

53 LEFT A text page from a 17th-century Chinese Qur'an. The decorative leaf functions as a marker, indicating the half way point in part six of a set originally in thirty volumes.
BL Or.15256/1, f. 30v.

54 A text page from a Javanese Qur'an written on local *dluwang* paper, early 19th-century. BL Add.12312, f. 198v.

in another *shamsah* medallion, where the lettering of the inscription ('I seek refuge in Allah from the accursed Satan') is reminiscent of Chinese dragons and snakes (fig. 51).

The adaptation of symbols common to Chinese art and culture is felt even more strongly in the final opening of a seventeenth-century Qur'an, where a lantern motif has become the visual vehicle for text in its decorated pages (fig. 52); the diamond at the centre of the lantern carries text which – as in the incipit pages and final openings of most Chinese Qur'ans – accommodates no more than three lines. Here the structure of the lantern is outlined in gold, the whole of which is set within a red double-lined rectangle. The impression of a Chinese lantern is further reinforced by pendulous tassels attached to the hooks on the outer side of the structures. Even textual markers can have a distinctive Chinese flavour as exemplified by the use of local flora in decorative designs (fig. 53).

Qur'ans from the Malay world
Islam was probably introduced to Indonesia and the Malay world by merchants from South India; it became firmly established there when the rulers of Pasai

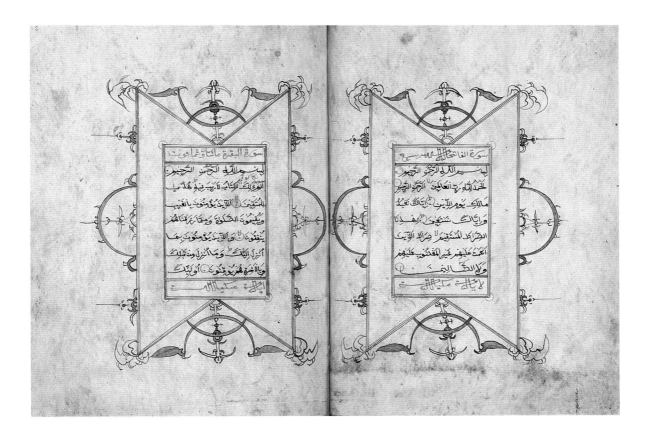

in North Sumatra converted in the thirteenth century, the religion of Islam spreading soon to other parts of the archipelago, the Malay Peninsula and Java included.

Qur'an manuscripts in the Malay world were written on paper. The paper used for Qur'ans in Java was of a particular kind called *dluwang* paper, made locally from the beaten bark of the mulberry tree. Typical of Javanese Qur'ans, the text is written in black ink with chapter headings in red (fig. 54). On the text pages of Javanese Qur'ans, the last few words (in black) of the preceding chapter are sometimes inserted in the heading panel of the next chapter. A feature of this page design is the placing of text within frameworks of finely ruled lines. By contrast, the decorated first opening of text is constructed within a starkly simple and abstract design, with each ornamental frame – dramatically outlined in black and red ink – fully symmetrical on a central axis (fig. 55). The text area on each page is enclosed within a lozenge with a v-shaped indentation at top and bottom; nonetheless, the simplicity of the design, with its restrained use of colour, is maintained and remains uncluttered, despite the ornamental tendrils and finials, and the large and small semi-circles which protrude into the margin.

55 The incipit pages of an early 19th-century Javanese Qur'an. BL Add.12312, ff. IV-2.

56 The incipit pages of a 19th-century Qur'an from the
East Coast of the Malay Peninsula. BL Or.15227, ff. 3v-4.

Unlike those from Java, Malay Qur'ans from the late sixteenth century on-wards were often produced on paper that had been manufactured in Europe. European paper was used here, as in other parts of the Muslim world, possibly because it was a trading commodity in the exchange of goods. In contrast to the paper made in the Middle East, which carried no markings, European paper was watermarked. The letters 'AG' are often found as watermarks in the paper of Malay Qur'ans. These are the initials of Andrea Galvani, the nineteenth-century Italian papermaker who worked in Pordenone, a centre of papermaking near Venice. A distinctive characteristic of Malay Qur'ans is seen in their use of vibrant colour as an integral part of the design. Particularly illustrative is a nine-teenth-century Qur'an from the East Coast of the Malay Peninsula with its broad range of colours, the most prominent of these being red, yellow, green and blue, with white for emphasis (fig. 56). In this first opening of the volume – containing chapter one and the beginning of chapter two – the text is encased in central panels. Typical of Qur'ans from this region, their rectangular frames are elaborately ornamented on three sides only, here with wave-like arches pro-truding into the margins. Again, as in China, local flora and vegetation appear to have been the inspiration for the stylized background of petals and leaves within the overall design. As for the text itself, the Arabic script has not been influenced by local calligraphy, as in the case of Chinese Qur'ans. The script is traditional *naskhi* in black, with yellow roundels to mark the end of each verse.

Sub-Saharan Qur'ans

Another distinct region of Islam, significant for the production of Qur'an man-uscripts, is the sub-Sahara and West Africa. In these areas Qur'ans were made to be portable, as they were generally carried by nomadic tribesmen. Hence, the leaves were generally unbound, not sewn together, but loose between boards, and thus more easily stored in a pouch or saddle bag (fig. 57). Like Malay Qur'ans, Qur'ans from sub-Saharan Africa were also produced on paper manufactured in Italy for export to the Muslim world. The text of these Qur'ans is written in *maghribi* script.

Possibly more representative of sub-Saharan Qur'ans is the manuscript written by a Hausa scribe from Nigeria (fig. 58). As in some *maghribi* Qur'ans from North Africa, the script is dense and compact leaving wide margins.

Invariably the text is in black ink, with chapter headings, vowel signs and other spelling symbols in red, and verse endings indicated by yellow circles. Text within ornaments is also inscribed in red. Here in the left-hand margin, the wording of the medallion (*sajdat Allah*) indicates when to prostrate during the recitation of the Qur'an.

In keeping with the practice of sub-Saharan scribes, the text of West African Qur'ans is also in black, again with chapter headings, vowel signs and spelling symbols in red (fig. 59). However, local colour-preference is strongly felt in the wide use of orange-red and yellow in round and semi-circular ornaments. The end of verses, too, is marked by yellow trefoils outlined in red, while yellow is also the colour for the letter *ha'*, here outlined in black, indicating the end of a fifth verse. Orange-red and yellow are also the dominant colours of the illuminated lattice panel which separates the chapters from each other. Yellow was possibly used because it is the nearest colour to gold and certainly less costly to obtain.

57 Loose leaves from a 19th-century West African Qur'an, with saddle bag. BL Or.13706.

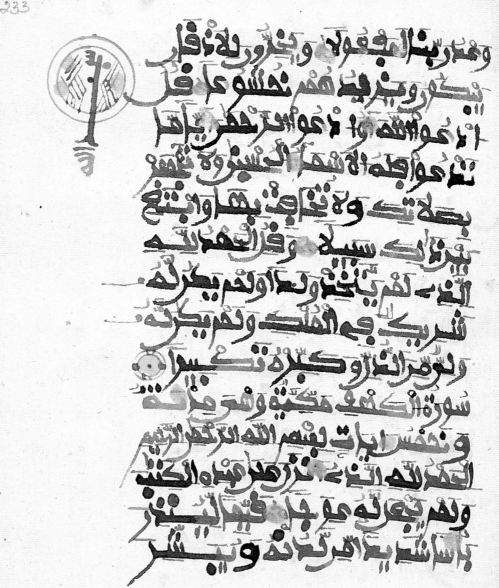

58 OPPOSITE A page from a Qur'an written by a Hausa scribe, sub-Sahara, 18th or 19th century. The yellow circles indicate verse endings. BL Or.6992, f. 233r.

59 ABOVE AND BELOW The loose, unbound, incipit pages of a 19th-century West African Qur'an. The illuminated lattice panel (below) separates the chapters. BL Or.13284, f.1v and 2r.

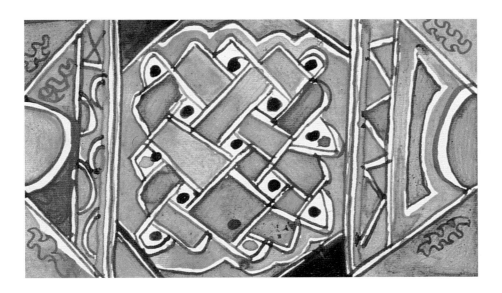

Miniatures, scrolls, bindings and furniture

From the Qur'ans we have seen so far – from different periods and parts of the Muslim world – one may have the impression that all Qur'ans are grand and monumental in scale. Miniature Qur'ans are no less distinctive for their decoration than for their format. Too small to be easily read, miniatures were usually carried by travellers as protective amulets and good luck charms, and were often encased in jewel-like boxes for safe keeping (fig. 61). Miniature Qur'ans come in various shapes – square, rectangular, often octagonal – and are written in a minute style of *naskhi* script known by the Arabic word for 'dust' (*ghubar*), the texture of the calligraphy being so fine that it is likened to powder (fig. 62). This script is particularly suitable for text that needs to be accommodated as neatly and as compactly as possible within the confines of a small page. As in large Qur'ans, the opening page of text is decorated. For example, in the first opening of a miniature Qur'an from the Ottoman period, the text is set in a central panel against a geometric ground (fig. 63). Here also, a gold diamond-shaped ornament, outlined in black on a sky-blue ground, is prominently featured in the panels at the top and bottom of the page. Adding to its richness, the framework is encased on three of its sides in gold strapwork, which itself is outlined in blue with blue spikes protruding into the margin.

60 OPPOSITE Characteristic of 17th-century Persian bookbinding is this Qur'an binding with an ornate floral panel blocked in gold at its centre. A prominent feature of the large central panel is the oval-shaped medallion with attendant pendants and cornerpieces.
BL Or.13279.

61 OPPOSITE TOP Miniature
Qur'an from Persia with gold
filigree cover and case in white
jade, 16th or 17th century.
BL Loth 36.

62 OPPOSITE BOTTOM
A miniature Qur'an written in a
minute style of *naskhi* script,
known as *ghubar* (dust), dated
950/1543, from Shiraz in Persia.
BL Or.2200, ff. 91v-92.

63 ABOVE The incipit pages
of a miniature Ottoman
Qur'an, inscribed in *ghubar*
(dust) script, 19th century.
BL Add.7222, ff. 1v-2 (enlarged).

Scrolls

Related to miniatures, in many ways, are those Qur'ans designed not as books, but as scrolls, which were possibly intended to be decorative rather than functional (fig. 64). These, too, are written in *ghubar* script to allow as much text as possible within a limited space. Although they contain the whole text of the Qur'an, these scrolls are not meant for recitation in prayer, since the script is not only too minuscule to be read but ingeniously arranged in decorative patterns designed to give visual impact to holy names and pious phrases.

Islamic bookbinding

Bookbinding has a long and ancient tradition. Its techniques and processes came to the attention of the Islamic world following the Arab conquest of Egypt in 641. The earliest Islamic bookbindings date from the ninth century and show markedly Coptic influences. Just as decoration and calligraphy can often suggest the place of origin of a Qur'an manuscript, so important clues can also be uncovered from its binding, particularly its ornamentation and style of tooling. Following religious doctrine and practice, the same non-figurative principles of Islamic art apply to the decoration of the binding as to the Qur'an manuscript itself; the designs are therefore generally geometric or at best floral. Although most Qur'an manuscripts were bound on completion, many original bindings have unfortunately not survived, having become detached from their pages and subsequently lost. As with calligraphy and illumination, much of what is known about Islamic bookbinding techniques is derived from general handbooks and manuals, as well as from individual treatises on the subject.

64 ABOVE The whole of the Qur'an written on a paper scroll for use as an amulet, Ottoman, 17th century. The writing on the scroll is arranged at various angles to form the pious expression, the *basmalah*, which reads 'In the name of God, the Merciful, the Compassionate'. BL IO Islamic 4150.

65 OPPOSITE A rare original Mamluk binding with flap, from the Qur'an commissioned by the Amir, Aytmish al-Bajasi, 14th century, Cairo. The central geometrical design (bottom) is typically Mamluk (detail, enlarged). BL Or.9671.

66 The binding of a 13th-century Qur'an from Marrakesh with blind
and gold tooling. This is the earliest known example of gold tooling
on a leather binding. BL Or.13192.

67 TOP AND ABOVE Binding of a 17th-century Persian Qur'an. The inscriptions,
embossed on sunken gold panels, are Sayings of the Prophet (see enlarged detail above).
BL Or.13279.

The sewing of the text block in Qur'an manuscripts was based on a Coptic technique using the chain-link stitch. Decorative endbands were not part of the primary sewing structure of the book but, when used, were generally made with two coloured threads tightly woven together. Unlike the bindings from Western Europe, which are typically clasped together, traditional Islamic bookbinding is characterized by a flap attached to the rear cover, which wraps around the leaves. This difference is illustrated by one of the few surviving masterpieces of binding on a Qur'an commissioned by the Amir Aytmish al-Bajasi (fig. 65). Here, the flap of the binding is wrapped round the fore-edge of the leaves, and tucked under the front cover of the book to protect the pages and keep them free from dust. The spine of the book is flat; there are no raised bands; and the edges of the binding do not overlap the pages. The binding in brown goatskin is incontestably Mamluk in style, especially the ornamentation of its central design, with gold tooling enhancing the focal point of the geometrical figure.

Although the practice of gold tooling flourished and reached a remarkable level of sophistication in Egypt during the Mamluk period, this technique is thought to have originated in Morocco. One of the earliest examples can be seen on the leather binding of a Qur'an copied in Marrakesh in 1256 (fig. 66). The central motif is a pattern of eight-pointed stars held together by an interlaced strapwork forming individual compartments. These are tooled in gold with an interlace of intricate ropework ornamented with dots and rosettes.

Some binding designs also incorporate panels for text inscriptions. A good example is a seventeenth-century Persian Qur'an, which carries in its Morocco binding Sayings of the Prophet (figs. 60 and 67). These are embossed on the sunken gold panels which surround the border. The central panel with its floral pattern is blocked in gold. This, together with an oval-shaped medallion forming the focal point at its centre, gives the binding the general effect of an ornate carpet page.

Qur'an furniture

As the sacred book of Islam, the text of the Qur'an was held in great respect. This is evident not only in the sensitivity of its calligraphy and illumination, but also in the manner in which the Qur'an volume itself is cared for. Generally speaking, single volume Qur'ans and multi-volume sets were stored in wooden cases or chests for safe-keeping. These often carried Qur'anic inscriptions and

68 The Qur'an open on the stand is volume seven of a ten-volume Qur'an. Copied about 1256 at Marrakesh, it is in the handwriting of the Almohad Sultan, Abu Hafs 'Umar al-Murtada (r. 1248–66). The original binding in blind and gold tooling appears in its entirety in plate 66.

were intricately decorated in gold, silver or mother-of-pearl. Another, and most practical, piece of Qur'an furniture is the Qur'an stand (figs. 68 and 69). This is not a lectern as used in the West, but a portable frame which, when set up, allows the Qur'an to be read while sitting cross-legged on the floor in study or at prayer. Ornate Qur'an stands were usually made of carved wood often embellished with mother-of-pearl.

69 PREVIOUS PAGE, ABOVE AND
OPPOSITE Qur'an stands from the
Ottoman period, decorated with
geometric patterns, pierced floral
designs and inlaid mother-of-pearl,
19th century.
BL Or.14617/1-3.

Further reading

Avrin, Leila, *Scribes, Script and Books, the Book Arts from Antiquity to the Renaissance* (Chicago and London, 1991).

Baker, Colin F, *Sultan Baybars' Qur'an*. CD Rom, The British Library, Turning the Pages (London, 2002).

Bayani, Manijeh, Contadini, Anna, and Stanley, Tim, *The Decorated Word. Qur'ans of the 17th to 19th Centuries*, The Nasser D. Khalili Collection of Islamic Art, vol. 4 (Oxford, 1999).

Bloom, Jonathan M., *Paper before Print, the History and Impact of Paper in the Islamic World* (Yale, 2001).

Brown, Michelle P., *The British Library Guide to Writing and Scripts, History and Techniques* (London, 1998).

Brown, Michelle P., *Understanding Illuminated Manuscripts, a Guide to Technical Terms* (London and Malibu, 1994).

Déroche, François, *The Abbasid Tradition. Qur'ans of the 8th to the 10th Centuries AD*, The Nasser D. Khalili Collection of Islamic Art, vol. 1 (Oxford, 1992).

Déroche (ed.), François, *Manuel de codicologie des manuscrits en écriture arabe* (Paris, 2000).

Déroche, François, 'Manuscripts of the Qur'an' in *Encyclopaedia of the Qur'an*, vol. 3, pp. 254–75 (Leiden, 2003).

Gaur, Albertine, *A History of Calligraphy* (London, 1994).

Guesdon, Marie-Geneviève, Vernay-Nouri, Annie (eds), *L'Art du livre arabe. Du manuscrit au livre d'artiste* (Paris, 2001).

Haldane, Duncan, *Islamic Bookbindings in the Victoria and Albert Museum* (London, 1983).

Islamic Arts Museum Malaysia, *The Message & the Monsoon, Islamic Art of Southeast Asia* (Islamic Arts Museum Malaysia, 2005).

Islamic Arts Museum Malaysia, *Six Centuries of Islamic Art in China* (Islamic Arts Museum Malaysia, 2001)

James, David, *Qur'ans and Bindings from the Chester Beatty Library* (London, 1980).

James, David, *Qur'ans of the Mamluks* (London, 1988).

James, David, *The Master Scribes. Qur'ans of the 10th to 14th Centuries AD*, The Nasser D. Khalili Collection of Islamic Art, vol. 2 (Oxford, 1992).

James, David, *After Timur. Qur'ans of the 15th and 16th Centuries AD*, The Nasser D. Khalili Collection of Islamic Art, vol. 3 (Oxford, 1992).

Karabacek, J. von, *Arab Paper* (London, 2001).

Khader, Salameh, *The Qur'an Manuscripts in the al-Haram al-Sharif Islamic Museum, Jerusalem* (Reading, 2001).

Kumar, Ann and McGlynn, John H., *Illuminations, the Writing Traditions of Indonesia* (Jakarta, New York and Tokyo, 1996).

Lewis (ed.), Bernard, *The World of Islam* (London, 1997 reprint)

Lings, Martin, *The Quranic Art of Calligraphy and Illumination* (London, 1976).

Lings, Martin and Safadi, Yasin Hamid, *The Qur'an* (London, 1976).

Safadi, Yasin Hamid, *Islamic Calligraphy* (London, 1978).

Index of manuscripts

Page numbers in italics refer to illustrations

General index

Page numbers in italics refer to illustrations